U.G.L.Y.

Uncovering God's Love for You

Stories of Triumph Over Low Self-Esteem

&

Self-Worth

EDITOR & CONTRIBUTING AUTHOR:

Sharva Hampton-Campbell

&

CONTRIBUTING AUTHORS:

Cynthia Cherry, Barbara Cook-Strong, Genesis Hall,
Sherri Hampton,
Anna Koomalsingh, Tina Mitchell, Jataun J. Rollins

&

Authrine T.K. Watson

DR NES INTERNATIONAL CONSULTING & PUBLISHING

LOS ANGELES, CA

U.G.L.Y.: Uncovering God's Love for You: Collective Stories of Triumph Over Low Self-Esteem & Self- Worth.

Dr. Nes International Consulting & Publishing
P.O. Box 70167
Pasadena, CA 91117
www.drnesintl.com

ISBN-1545577811

The book recounts certain events in the lives of the authors: Cynthia Cherry, Barbara Cook-Strong, Genesis Hall, Sherri Hampton, Sharva Hampton-Campbell, Anna Koomalsingh, Tina Mitchell, Jataun J. Rollins & Authrine T.K. Watson, according to their recollection and perspective. While all the stories are true, some names and identifying details have been changed to protect the privacy of those involved.

Publisher's Note: The sole purpose of these stories is to uplift and empower the readers and not defame any parties involved. All content was given on part of the authors and in no way, represent the views, perspective, or eye witness account of the publisher or publishing company.

Front and back cover design by Chanelle Renee-www.chanellerenee.com

Dedication

This book is dedicated to every woman who has experienced circumstances in their lives that left them feeling vulnerable, unsure of themselves, unworthy or less than. Life throws us many curve balls; many of which we miss or strike out, but there are a few in which we hit a home run. The missed balls and strike outs are nothing more than God letting you know that He is still perfecting you. This book is about uncovering God's love for you. He's perfecting you out of love and adoration. As daughters of the King, he wants us to prosper. This includes emotional, physical and spiritual well-being; as well as finances. As you read each of the stories, take note of how I, along with these women used our faith in God to overcome some events and situations that negatively impacted our self-esteem and self-worth. We triumphed over each obstacle and in doing so we are strong enough to share our stories with you. We are the Women of Ushindi!!!!

Contents

1

U-G-L-Y

by

Sharva Hampton-Campbell

*U*GLY, *you ugly, yea, you ugly!!!* This was the chant we shouted at the opposing team during our high school basketball games. They would respond, "Yo mamma, yeah, yeah, yo mamma!" The back and forth would continue until someone had enough sense to start another chant. This type of cheering was considered "in your face" chants to let the opposing team know that our team was not afraid of them. After reminiscing about the days of old, I began researching the origins or this chant. Low and behold, I found that what we chanted was a small stanza of the actual cheer. It blew my mind; let's see if you get the same reaction:

U.G.L.Y. you ain't got no alibi you ugly eh! Hey! You ugly!
I saw you walking down the street just the other day
I didn't see your damage from that far away
I should have got a clue when the kids started screaming

You walked up to me with your buck teeth a gleaming
Your hair was all frizzy and your face was a mess
I thought it was a sack but it's your favorite dress
You hurt the trees feelings and the birds all flew
I don't mean to insult you
Oh wait! Yes, I do.

Your teeth are yellow, they're covered in mold
You're only fourteen you look a hundred years old
When looks were handed out you were last in line
Your face looks like where the sun don't shine
Did you fall off a building and land on your head
Or did a truck run over your face instead
There ain't no pill cos you ain't ill
You're ugly!

U.G.L.Y you ain't got no alibi you ugly eh! Hey! You ugly!
What you really need is to wear a mask
And book that plastic surgeon fast - (girl)
You're scary - you're hairy I heard about you
You're the main attraction at the city zoo
You're so fat and ugly with a belly full of flab
When you wear a yellow coat people shout out cab
(so funny)
You got eyes like a pig and your nose is big
And with hair like that you should be wearing a wig
Uncle Fester remember him? I never knew that you had a twin
You can't disguise your googly eyes
In the miss ugly pageant you win first prize
Yo mama says you ugly -
You ugly!

U.G.L.Y you ain't got no alibi you ugly eh! Hey! You ugly!
Get busy (x15)
Yo mama says you're ugly
Get busy

6

Yo mama says you're ugly
Get busy
Yo mama says you're ugly
Get busy you're ugly!
U.u.u.u.
Now i feel like blondie
U.G.L.Y you ain't got no alibi you ugly eh! Hey! You ugly!
Quasimodo
Camel breath
Squarehead
Ugly!
Chicken legs
Pig face
Chin like bubba
Ugly!
Fish lips
Toad licker
Poindexter
Ugly!
Spaghetti arms
Limp butt
Freak show - ugly!
U.G.L.Y you ain't got no alibi you ugly eh! Hey! You ugly!
U.G.L.Y - you could make an onion cry
U.G.L.Y - like an alien chased by the F.B.I.
U.G.L.Y x6
U.G.L.Y you ain't got no alibi you ugly![1]

I cannot imagine repeating these lyrics to someone! I do not believe there is truth to the children's rhyme on how, "Sticks and stones may break my bones, but words will

---

[1] http://www.lyricsplanet.com/lyrics.php?id=8698 Retrieved on January 18, 2017.

never hurt me." I can recall many times in my life where the cruel and insensitive words of others hurt me to the core. This was especially true during my childhood. In finding myself, I questioned why my hair was so nappy, why was my skin the darkest of my family members, why was I always the tallest in my class and more importantly, why was my legs so skinny and my knees knocked? I did not come to these discoveries on my own, my peers at school made me aware of them. They teased me about my hair being nappy. I was no stranger to the pressing comb, but there was one major flaw in getting my hair fried, dyed and laid to the side (a flashback memory of the hot comb) every two weeks. My hair sweated back to its original nappy (or kinky) state within a day or so because of the hot and very humid weather in Louisiana.

I was born in Bogalusa, Louisiana and was raised there during my formative years. Can you imagine leaving the hairdresser or beauty shop with beautiful silky straight hair and two days later, it transformed into a gigantic puff of coiled hair sprawled all over your head? Well, this was my experience. I could hear my mother's voice, "You better not sweat your hair back before church on Sunday." She talked like I had control over the humidity and heat index. She had somehow forgotten that we did not have the luxury of central air in our home. Plus, we were frequently told to go outside and play after chores were complete.

Outside play was much more rigorous than that of today's youth. We played *Tag, Red Light Green Light, Red Rover*, and *Mother May I*. Jumping rope and hopscotch were also avid games we played until our pre-teens days. The physical exertion required to endure these games would result in profuse sweating. I guess, if I had been a "girly girl" I would have sat under the juniper tree and played with my tea set or read books. Nope, that was all boring to me! Soon, things changed. My mother gave me a relaxer. I was SO glad when my mother gave me a relaxer! That was the end of being called a nappy head!

One level of taunts ended but, another one began! I was now being called "Blacky," "Smut face," Chocolate Drop," "Juju Monster" and "Tar Baby" because of my dark completion. This was a horrible time during my childhood because it was something I could not control. I had to endure it. The most hurtful time of all was when one of my light-skinned cousins called me a "Black Bitch." We were sitting at the foot of my mother's bed watching a wrestling match between Junk Yard Dog (JYD) and Ted Dibiase (TD). I told her I was rooting for JYD and she responded, "So, he ain't gonna win." I said, "Yes he is!" JYD won and she became furious because I was taunted her about the win. After a few minutes of me saying, "I told you so." She looked at me and said, "You make me sick, you Black Bitch!" Immediately I responded, "I have tolerated name calling from strangers and peers, but I be damned if I am going to take this from you! Let me show you what a Black Bitch looks like!" I began punching and kicking her in the stomach, arms and legs until bruises started to appear everywhere. She had become my punching bag because she did not fight back. Instead, she tried to block my punches and get away. Eventually, I pinned her down on the bed. I hit her until I got tired. Then I threatened her and told her she better not tell the truth about how she actually got the bruises. She was very clumsy, so I told her to say she fell while playing. I knew our parents would believe her.

I remember being very close to one of my maternal uncles. He was my favorite uncle. He and I had the darkest skin color of all my family. I truly believe that this commonality was the center of our strong connection. When I met my father, he was not as dark as me. My siblings are not as dark as me either. There was a juke joint in the neighborhood where I grew up and I remember hearing some of the men and women entering and exiting the place refer to me as being, "a pretty little black girl." After hearing this, I thought, "why couldn't I just be a pretty little girl?" They were not referring to my race because they were black as well; instead, I knew they were referring to the tone of my skin. As I got older, I remember when I heard the saying, "The blacker the berry, the sweeter the juice." I thought it meant something good and would repeat it when someone called me a name that referenced the tone of my skin until I learned that this prose had a different meaning. It means that the darker your skin color, the sweeter is your juice.[2] So, I had to stop using this phrase as a "come back" statement.

Still there was more for me to battle. It was as if having two strikes against myself was not enough, nappy hair and dark skin were not the only flaws that I was teased about. My height soon became an issue for me too! I was always the tallest in my class, and I can remember back to kindergarten when we had to line up for everything, to go to the bathroom, to go to the auditorium for assemblies, to go to lunch, to go to recess, even to go outside to practice fire and hurricane

---

[2] http://www.urbandictionary.com/define.php?term=the%20black er%20the%20berry%20the%20sweeter%20the%20juice&utm_sour ce=search-action Retrieved on January 18, 2017.

drills. I was always the last one. The taunt was "shorty first and tall gal last." For a while, I thought my name was "tall gal" because I had been referenced by it so much. Being last did not provide any incentives; in fact, it seemed to be a curse. In the lunchroom, they would run out of chocolate milk by the time I got to the beverage counter. By the time I made it outside to recess, I didn't seem to have as much time to play with the other kids, and worst of all was by the time I got to go to the bathroom I would have almost wet my pants.

Junior high brought with it an entirely different set of issues! As a 12-year-old, not only was I still the tallest, but I was a thick girl too! During this time, thin was in, and I just didn't fit in. The boys liked to shoot marbles with me and play tag, but they never put their arms around my waist and walked me to class or tried to steal a kiss or make a flirtatious move. I remember getting into a fight with this girl group that called themselves "The Gangstas" and I remember fighting them by myself, while my best friend stood by and watched with a fearful look on her face. I was told afterwards that I made a roaring sound and began swinging and hitting them as they charged at me. *The Incredible Hulk* television series had recently aired, and after the fight, my peers started calling me the *Incredible Hulk*. They said during the encounter, my body turned green, I made an ugly face and roared like the *Incredible*

Hulk just before I beat up "The Gangstas." While I was glad that I had defended myself, and knew "The Gangstas" would never bother me again, the embarrassment caused by the constant teasing ensued. To make matters worse, the most horrific incident occurred while I was walking to the library at school to work on a class project. A group of my classmates was leaving the library and proceeding to walk down the hallway. When they saw me, they yelled, "Run, run for your lives! Here comes the *Incredible Hulk*!" One of the guys threw up his arms like the Hulk and made a roaring sound. Afterward, they all started laughing and running in the opposite direction. I scurried into the library to find an isolated, quiet spot. I cried intensely. After about three months the Hulk stuff died out, and others became the focus of peer teasing and taunting. But I wasn't out of the woods just yet!

During my last year in Junior high school, short skirts were fashionable. I wanted to make a statement and fit in. I learned to sew in Home Economics class, so I would make different pieces of clothing and wear them to school. This time, I made a mini skirt. I wore it to school with much pride and admiration! On the way to school, I noticed my peers at the bus stop whispering and laughing, but I didn't pay any attention to what they were talking about. It *never* crossed my mind that they were talking about me!

When we arrived at school, I got off the bus and proceeded to walk towards my locker. I heard laughing and saw my peers pointing in my direction. I immediately start to wonder if my panties were showing or perhaps I had tissue hanging out of my skirt. I couldn't even image that they were laughing at my skirt because I knew I had been very meticulous in cutting out the pattern and sewing it. Nope, I was wrong! I heard someone say, "She got chicken legs and she knock-kneed." My immediate thoughts were, "I wish I could disappear." I opened my locker and buried my face in there for a quick second. I told myself, "Don't you cry and ignore them." One of my girlfriends came to my rescue and blurted out, "Y'all just jealous! Don't be haters!" I'll never forget how her support made me feel! But, I couldn't wait until school was over and to get home!

My house was my world; it was a safe place to be me, the nappy headed, tall black girl with knocked-knees. My house was my place of refuge. I was accepted at home, no matter how different I was from the rest of my family. I was accepted, and that's where I wanted to escape to my place of unconditional acceptance. The school day was finally over! I got off the school bus, which was about three blocks from my house. With a backpack full of books, and all the strength I could muster in my legs, I literally ran all the way home! When I arrived, I opened the door and yelled for my mother. "Momma, Momma, I hate that school," I said. She came hurriedly to the front door, and I began to sob in her arms. When I finally calmed down, I began to collect my words and gather myself. I spilled it all out! I told her about how horrible my day had been. Soon, I begin to reveal to her about the name calling I had endured since kindergarten. She looked at me in amazement and stated that she had no idea that I had been dealing with such foolishness. She reassured me that she would have talked to my peers' parents and the school counselor. Then, she motioned me to the living room and told me to sit down on the couch. She left the room and returned with her Bible. She read aloud to me, Psalm 139:4 "I will praise thee; for I am fearfully and wonderfully made: marvelous are thy works; and that my soul knoweth right well" (KJV). After which, she told me that God created us to be unique in His image and likeness. She explained that everyone had flaws that God sees as beauty and no one has a right to tease anyone about how God created them. We should embrace each other's differences because we are the creative works of God. Her words were very comforting. As she spoke them, I felt a renewing in my mind about who I was as a Child of God. I wanted everyone to see me as God saw and created me, but I had to come to the realization that everyone would not, and I had to be ok with that realization. I went to school the next day with my head held high, and from that day forward when I was teased, I would tell them what thus sayeth the Lord according to Psalm 139:4.

Initially, when I repeated what my mother told me or the Bible verse, my peers would start laughing and walk away. Eventually, the teasing stopped and other classmates that were victims of verbal bullying and taunting began asking me how to make it stop. I told them to try to ignore it and if they could not they needed to talk to their parents and the school counselor for support. I made it through middle school and high school brought about another set of issues. However, I was emotionally ready and mature for high school. I had prepared all summer long to be confident in who I was as a beautiful creation of God. In the eleventh grade, I tried out for the Pom- Pom squad. At 201 pounds and 5'10" tall, I made the team! This really upset some of the smaller petite girls who did not make the team. I was so proud to represent the "big girls," as we were often called.

Throughout my young adult life, I was faced with situations in which peers and on several occasions boyfriends who tried to ridicule me by referencing my skin color or my size and each time I laughed and said, "that's all you got?" They could not understand why their words did not break me and I did not have time to explain. I would laugh and walk away leaving them perplexed.

Ultimately, there are only two outcomes in how we use our words. We can use them to tear each other down or build each other up. I challenge you to be a person who build people up with your words and tear down their use of name calling and taunting by showing them that you are confident in who you are as a person. How do you gain confidence in yourself? I am so glad you ask.   Get a mirror and look at yourself.   Look at your face, its outline, your eyes, eyebrows, eyelashes, nose, mouth, ears, cheeks, forehead, and chin.   Move on down to the other parts of your body looking at each part until you have a full mental picture of you, then tell yourself, *I am fearfully and wonderfully made. I am a treasure and beauty in the eyesight of God. He crafted every part of my me in His likeness and for His glory; not to be subjected to personal self-destruction or to be judged by others.*

If you are experiencing teasing, taunting or verbal abuse by a peer or loved one, please talk to someone whom you trust to help you process your feelings and build your confidence of who you are as a person, as well as help you determine how to end the abuse.   These types of situations can weigh heavily on you emotionally, oft times causing you to doubt who you are as a person. Your self-worth can become diminished. We all have value and worth. Think about your talents and gifts. These are God-given entities that provide us with a sense of validation. If you have not discovered your gifts and talents, I ask you to answer this question and by doing so it will point you in the right direction for discovery. What are those things that you naturally do well and they bring you joy? Now, activate them and SOAR!!

This is how I maintain a high level of confidence in who I am and whose I am. I have cultivated my gifts and talents to uplift and strengthen others and in turn there is a reciprocal sustaining of my self-esteem and self-worth.

About the Author

Sharva Hampton-Campbell has a passion and zeal for helping women tap into their God-given purpose. She accomplishes this through life coaching sessions that focus on personal and professional development using biblical principles. She is a licensed minister who enjoys helping ministries develop programs that enrich the lives of its congregation. Having obtained a Bachelor's and Master's Degrees in Social Work from the University of Illinois at Urbana-Champaign, Mrs. Hampton-Campbell's educational background has afforded her opportunities to work in various settings in which the lives of women, children and families were vastly improved. She has traveled stateside and internationally as a motivational speaker where the lives of women were immensely enriched. Her most memorable experience was having the opportunity to sit in the chambers of the Prime Minister of Trinidad and Tobago's office sharing with him information about her workshop topic, "Connecting Inspiration and Spirituality," in which she was preparing to facilitate the following day along with a group of professional women.

Sharva is the founder of Azinza, a women's organization that host annual empowerment retreats. She is also the founder of Women on the Move Network, a women's organization that serves to help the lives of those in need. A true trailblazer who also founded and operated several agencies, a nonprofit organization called The Carol Lizzy Empowerment Zone and an incorporated organization called The YES Mentoring Program. Both businesses provided resources and services to disenfranchised youth and their families.

Sharva has co-authored "Becoming the Professional Woman," "The Young Woman's Guide for Personal Success," "The Christian Women's Guide for Personal Success," and "Survival Skills for The African-American Woman." She has a children's book and a personal memoir that are currently in publication. She believes that writing is central to the healing process. It provides a cathartic experience that propels you to wholeness. A native of Louisiana, Sharva currently resides in Champaign, Illinois with her husband of twenty-five years.

2

SURVIVING LIFE'S STORMS
by
Tina Mitchell

Growing up was difficult for me. I am the youngest of five children. There is a large age difference between me and my siblings. There is ten years between me and my brother and sister, and almost twenty years between me and my two older brothers. I felt awkward as a child because all my friends' brothers and sisters were close in age to them. I enjoyed school growing up. I always made good grades and was on honor roll.

However, the toughest part about growing up was my mom's medical condition. It caused her to be hospitalized repeatedly during my young and adult years. So, while most girls grow up playing in their mom's make-up and heels, I missed out on all those experiences. My dad raised me while my Mom was in the hospital. My sister lived with and was raised by my Granny, so I did not get to experience the bond between sisters, like most girls.

I remember a time I wanted to be in *Girl Scouts* and I needed my mother's consent, but it was one of those times my mom was hospitalized. I was devastated. My brother's girlfriend saw how hurt I was and how much I really wanted to be a *Girl Scout*. She stepped in and signed my consent form and even purchased my uniform. This made me happy!

By this time, I reached 6th grade, there was another turn of events. Not only did I feel lonely about not having my mom around, now I was losing my brother to prison. This really affected me because now I wanted to try-out for basketball, but I was not allowed to try-out because my mom was in the hospital and my brother was in prison. I was angry with my dad, because I felt I was being punished because of my brother's actions and because of my mom illness. It just did not seem fair! Along with dealing with this, I was humiliated by the other children on the school bus. They teased me because of the beauty mark on my face. They called it a *black booger*. All the neighborhood children laughed and made fun of me.

I felt all alone and isolated. I felt ashamed and did not have anyone to rely upon. I believed no one truly understood how I felt inside. Imagine growing up, and every time you looked around your mom was in and out of the hospital. This had a devastating impact on me, as a child. I did not fully understand the reality of what happened. Now, as I reflect, I feel it's the worst thing you can hide from a child. It is best to sit them down and educate them on what is happening. Since I didn't know or understand what was occurring, I internalized it, and believed I was to blame for my mom's hospitalization. I believed she was there because I was a bad girl. I would pray to God and say, "God, if you make my mom well, I promise I won't be bad again." It was not until I was in college that I stop blaming myself, and understood that mom was experiencing a chemical imbalance of the brain.

I remember writing a paper during my psychology class, regarding the role of medication. My instructor wrote a note on my paper stating that the paper was well written, but to never blame myself. I took that psychology class in 1994, and those words she wrote then, I have never forgotten. By 1998, my mother was hospitalized again. By then, I had become accustomed to her hospitalizations. I saw this often as a child, now as an adult, things were a bit different. I went from being oblivious to her situation to investigating everything that concerned her. I questioned everyone that was involved in my mom's care. The receptionist, nurses, health technicians, licensed clinical social workers, and the doctors all heard my concerns. Even the pharmacists heard from me! Soon, the researcher in me began to blossom. I started going to the library checking out book after book, after book, reading up on my Mom's condition. I became an advocate for my mom and spoke for her when she couldn't make decisions for herself. This empowered me! As a child, I couldn't make decisions on behalf of mom, but as an adult, I sought lots of answers.

Beyond this, I gained a great respect for my dad. He honored his marriage vows, as he loved and cared for my mom, "in sickness and in health." He could have easily turned his back on my mom, and placed her in an institution when the doctor told him she would never be well. However, he did not listen and found another doctor to help her. Once, there was a time when the doctor prescribed too much medication for my mom, it nearly killed her! The doctor lost his license and no longer in practice. Soon, my Granny helped my dad find another doctor. I was devastated by this situation. I felt completely helpless. We wanted mom to be well, but could not seem to help her. We had to trust the doctors. Sometimes many of the health professionals did not have mom's best interest in mind. I learned that some professionals like to experiment on patients who have adequate insurance until they can find the right combination of medicines. I thought this entire ordeal was unfair. My Mom never drank or did any illegal drugs, so why did she have to experience these issues? Watching my Mom go through the intensity of her illness, in turn made me sad. During one visit with Mom, my brother came in and my Mom told the nurse he was her special son, her oldest son, and she wanted him to have the best of everything. I sat there speechless. While I was excited that she felt this way about him, my feelings were hurt because my Mom always professed that she loved us "all the same."

Soon, Mom came home after a month and somehow needed to go right back! It was tough! This time it was this technician on duty, he called dad, my youngest brother, and I into another room. He questioned why she returned to the hospital and asked if we had considered a long-term care facility. He expressed to us that he had not seen any improvement in Mom during her former stay and we should consider long term options. Dad immediately responded, "She's not going to a nursing home!" I admired my dad. He was adamant about taking care of *his* wife. There was a slow road to recovery, but I believed in the biblical text that states, "with God all things are possible (Mark 10:27). I remained prayerful. Mom's journey is an awesome living testimony of what God will do despite what nurses, technicians, and doctors predicted.

In 2004, mom's doctor retired. After a couple years, this shift in providers and medicines caused mom to relapse. By 2007, mom was hospitalized again. I was working full time. Dad was convinced that mom was not receiving the proper care, so he took her out of the hospital and cared for her at home. I shifted my work schedule so I could help care for Mom. I remember needing to teach my mom basic life skills, all over again. This was a long tedious process.

While many people shy away from it, or are ashamed to talk about these issues, mental illness is real. It's a reality for millions of Americans. It's time to become transparent about these issues, so individuals are no longer stigmatized and receive adequate help. Additionally, there should be assistance provided for the caregivers as well. The sacrifices they make to care for others impacts their lives greatly as well. I wanted to share some of my experiences here, so others who are going through the same thing would know ultimately, there is hope.

However, the emotionality of all of this impacted me greatly. Later I sought love in places that were detrimental. In 2009, I started dating a nice, tall, good looking well-dressed man of God. We would always have fun together. He was charming and full of surprises. As a matter of fact, our first date was a shopping spree. I received a new wardrobe while shopping at some of the finest stores out of town. Later, we spent time traveling to surrounding cities St. Louis, Chicago, Champaign, and Springfield for nice entertainment. We went to the Cardinals baseball game, Gospel Fest events, and various musical concerts. We were enjoying life!

Soon, the fun started to cease. One day, I received an anonymous phone call from a woman about him. He basically blew it off as a jealous woman seeking to hurt me. But, that one woman turned into two, then three. More and more people would provide me with different information about him. I guess I was naïve. I did not want to believe the things people were suggesting. We continued traveling together. However, after attending a cruise conference, I had decided that I wanted to end our relationship. When I got back in town, I went into the bedroom where he was and said, "I don't think we should be together anymore." He was very emotional and started crying and asked me if this was what I really wanted to do. I fell for the tears. It made me think he really did care for me, and he was serious about our relationship. He asked my dad for my hand in marriage. Despite, receiving more information about him, we moved forward.

In 2010, we received our marriage license. That same night he proposed at a local Japanese steakhouse. Shortly following, we started our official marriage counseling sessions. Then a month later, we celebrated together in holy matrimony. We left for our honeymoon. It was supposed to be the happiest time of my life, but things went from bad to worse. Two weeks later, we ran into one of my guy friends while vacationing. I introduced him to my husband and we

26

caught up a bit. Before I knew it, he and my husband had gotten into an argument. I tried my best to end the argument. After experiencing the incident, we went back to the hotel room. Once we got there, we argued and the beginning of the mental cruelty commenced. Two weeks following, as we were in bed together, my husband looked and me and yelled, "I hate women!" I laid there, dumbfounded. He continued, "women are complicated creatures!" I began to think, "What had I gotten myself into?" During the times, I wanted to be intimate, he told me that, "I could get it from somewhere else, if he was not giving me enough." It got bad! During times he was upset, he would sleep in our guest room. Soon, physical abuse started. He pushed me on several occasions. One time, he choked me in bed because I wanted to talk and he did not. Verbal abuse was not too far behind. On several occasions, he would curse me out or belittle me, and complain about what I cooked. He would get mad when I chewed gum or ice because he could not stand the crunching sound. As you can probably tell, he was very controlling. Once we were married, he forced me to cancel my phone service and share a plan with him. When he was mad with me, he would disable my ability to send text messages. Eventually, he turned my phone service off and told me that I cost him $125 since I got my own phone through a different company. Next, he cut the home internet service off. It seemed that if it was not one thing, it surely was another!

During the dating phase, everything was good. He was the perfect gentlemen. We did everything together, but once we got married it all changed. As a newlywed, I desired to be with my husband all the time. I did not want him to be gone on business all the time, especially early in the marriage. There were several events I went to alone. As time went, the abuse continued. On one occasion, we had argued after leaving a guest church and he hit me in my face. How can someone hit the person that they are supposed to love? In my heart, I knew it was not going to work, but I tried my best to reject that reality. There I was married to a minister and I had experienced more abuse from him than I ever did from the ordinary man from the streets! This was surely not my expectations of what married life was supposed to be! I did look at the example of my parents. There were married 57 years, and I had never heard of dad abusing my mom. My dad was the epitome of love and dedication, especially during her time of illness.

I remember times we were in bed and my husband's phone would vibrate at unusual times. Coupled with the various allegations that various people made to me, it all made me suspicious. Soon I began to not trust my husband. One day, I decided to check his phone. This is where I will now advise everyone. Do not go looking for something, because you will find it and you might not be able to handle it. I got much more than what I bargained for! There were several inappropriate texts. I found "Do you want some?" "My place or yours," "I need another $100 or I go to Wifey" and "Hey Boo I was sleep when you called last night." All these texts were from other men. I clearly could not handle this. I kept his phone. He asked for his phone. It was all, too much! I was so distraught. I told him that I threw his phone in the lake. His response, "You should have driven your car in the lake, instead. It would have been better for the both of us!" This was the lowest blow. I couldn't take anymore! This was the ultimate form of rejection by my husband. Finally, I had reached the point I thought I could not take it anymore. By this time, I was afraid of the embarrassment and became consumed and concerned about what others would think. I thought of myself as a failure. I did not want to live anymore. That evening, I went in the bedroom and took a bottle of sleeping pills. I'm not sure how much time passed, but I was rushed to the hospital by ambulance. The sleeping pills were pumped out of my system, and I had to have a blood transfusion. I was released the next day. He picked me up from the hospital and I came home to a husband being very upset.

He continued to minister at other local churches, and our home persisted to be a living hell. I remember one night we were supposed to attend a local event to honor my Uncle, but we never made it. We fought, I'll never forget that night! He grabbed me, pushed me, and yelled as I fell to the ground, "take some pills while I am gone!" The door slammed shut behind him. Later, he came back into the house and made it clear that he no longer wanted to be married.

The shocking reality that our brief marriage was about to end, was not something I wanted to easily accept. Things began to spiral further out of control. My husband changed the lock to our home. I had to get the police involved, to which he did not agree. He moved all my belongings to my parents' house while I was at work. Eventually, we finalized our divorce. I attempted counseling, as it was a grievous time for me.

I know most people will ask why did I stay in such a chaotic situation. I guess, I thought life would be better or as the saying goes, I thought the grass was greener on the other side. It is hard when someone is so nice while you are dating, they are prominent and well respected in the community, but turn into a different character behind closed doors.

I suffered in silence. I smiled in public, but I was hurting deep down inside. One thing for sure, you must love yourself before anyone else can. Most importantly, love God because God is love. Do not ever allow anyone to have so much control over you. Do not allow bad situations or circumstances to make you bitter. I harbored a lot of hurt and resentment towards my mom and my brother for years because I thought my life would have turned out differently or better if it had not been for them.

While attending church one Sunday, God spoke to me through a sermon from my pastor. He said it was important to forgive and not to be mad with my parents because they have raised me the best they knew how. I have learned to accept circumstances of life as learning experiences and become better. As my Bishop says, *better is on the way*! Your attitude determines your altitude. Now that I am free from bondage, I have that true loving family relationships. Do not ever give up on family.

I thank God for His grace and mercy. It is important to have a personal relationship with God. Pray. Read and study the scriptures daily. When I felt weak, the God in me was still strong and would not let me be defeated. I shall live and not die! I am so thankful for the many prayers that went out for me. God placed God-fearing powerful praying people in my life to speak into me and over me. He even used my brother who is not a Christian to encourage me to get me out of that low feeling I was in. My cousin prayed with me every single morning, in the wee hours of the morning when everyone else was asleep. My sister would always tell me to "keep it moving." My nephew texted me, "that this minor setback is actually a setup for a major comeback." My mentor reminded me to get it together and to focus on God and not my problems. Trust in the Lord with all thine heart; and lean not unto thine own understanding. In all thy ways acknowledge him, and he shall direct thy paths (Proverbs 3:5-6) is a scripture that helped me through.

In closing, I want to offer this advice. Do not let anyone control your emotions by their actions and always let the Holy Spirit guide your feelings. Keep a positive faith filled attitude because God is in control. Walk in forgiveness daily.

I hope by me sharing my story, uncovering the mask, uncovering my hurt, and uncovering God's love for me will help you get free. Despite the myth and stigma, mental illness and thoughts of not wanting to live are real, even with in the black community. Thank God, I survived! There are many who do not live to tell of the goodness of God. It is easy for some Christians to put on a front, but deep down many are hurt and broken. Going to church and saying the right things are not enough. So many are sitting in church Sunday after Sunday suffering but afraid to speak up and ask for help because they feel they will be ostracized. We must become servants, pray for others, and extend help to the ordinary common people not just those who are popular and well known. For God so loved the world that he gave his only begotten Son, that whosoever believeth in him should not perish, but have everlasting life, (John3:16). So, in uncovering God's love for you, I leave you with these final scriptures: "Thou shalt love the Lord thy God with all thy heart and with all thy soul, and with all thy mind. This is the first and great commandment. And the second is like unto it, thou shalt love thy neighbor as thyself (Matthew 22: 37-39). Forgiveness is the key to walking in your victory.

Though I was involved in a failed marriage and I did not want to live anymore, I know that everything I have experienced is not just for me. It is for God to get the glory! There is great power which comes from surviving the storm. Whatever storm that you are experiencing, keep pushing, pray and trust that God will see you through every step of the way. Surround yourself with the right people, and believe that you're worth fighting for. You are a person of triumph and victory!

About the Author

Tina Mitchell is a native of Decatur, Illinois. She is the youngest of five children. She's a loving daughter, sister, cousin, aunt, and friend. She is a member of the Antioch Missionary Baptist Church and attends Life Changers Church. She has previously attended Chicago Baptist Institute (Decatur Satellite Campus) working towards a Bachelor degree in Christian Education. She's the first in her family to attend and graduate with high honors from Richland Community College with A.A.S. in Office Technology. Tina began her career with Kroger in 1993. She's been an Independent Avon Representative since 1998. Tina likes to travel and go to concerts.

3

MIRROR, MIRROR
by
Cynthia Cherry

STILL UGLY

It was winter break at Western Illinois University, my undergraduate college. My friend and I lived in family housing, we didn't have to adhere to the off-campus restrictions for the dorms. We were in no rush to leave campus like most students, so we took our time packing with plans to leave later in the day. My friend hadn't been feeling well that day. I suggested that she go to the hospital upon our arrival in Chicago. We left Macomb, Illinois at five that evening and three hours or so later we were entering Interstate 94 en route to the Westside of Chicago. I took over driving once we made it to the city limits. We headed straight to then, *Cook County Hospital's*[3] emergency room off California Avenue. We were full-time students, we couldn't

---

[3] In 2001, *Cook County Hospital* was changed to *John H. Stroger Jr Hospital of Cook County.* http://articles.chicagotribune.com/2001-12-19/news/0112190151_1_stroger-new-hospital-richard-phelan Retrieved December 24, 2016.

afford health insurance, and so going to the county hospital was her only option for avoiding a bill.

It was a little after 1 a.m. by the time we left the emergency room (the sacrifice you make for free health care service). My friend was diagnosed with the flu, given a prescription and released with some basic aftercare instructions. Walking out of the emergency room at 1 in the morning, the streets were vacant, not a soul insight. Completely unaware that we were being watched as we walked towards the car, my friend and I argued over who was going to drive us home. "Give me this chain you ugly B---(he pushes the gun against my side) and snatches one of two of the gold herringbone necklace from my neck. "Who you calling ugly"? You B---, now shut the F--- up and come up out them chains and rings." "Man, I ain't giving you nothing punk, calling me ugly.," I retorted! "B-----, is you crazy (as he points the gun to my face)? I will blow yo Mother F----- brains out! "Cent, shut up and give him the chain before you get us killed," my friend screamed. I guess I didn't move fast enough, as I was taking off my rings, he snatches the second necklace off my neck, leaving a nasty scratch. My friend wasn't wearing any jewelry but she politely offered her *Dooney and Bourke* purse, which he snatched out her hand, as he ran off into the darkness.

"He got some nerves calling me ugly!" I said, as my friend sped down California Avenue towards the "E way" (express way). We passed the Chicago Police Department, not a cop insight! My friend was silent; she was *still* in shock; after all, we just got robbed in front of a hospital and could have lost our lives! Meanwhile, I was sulking that the stick-up man called me ugly. Tears began to roll down my cheeks as I thought to myself "surely I was over this by now." But it was obvious that I was still an ugly duckling.

I was 19 years old, a single mother, surviving my second semester of college when that happened. I had been fighting to overcome a lot of insecurities in my life and just in that one moment a stranger managed to send me back to a place I feared the most by uttering the words "YOU UGLY." He threw a grenade and blew up my fort. The shadows of my childhood insecurities of being the "ugliest girl of them all" emerged. Never mind the fact that I could have lost my life! The realization that I had succumbed to my insecurities again angered me. Whoever came up with saying of "stick and stone may break my bone but words will never hurt me" is a LIE! In my world, those words cut me like a knife without an anesthesia. That day, I had learned that all I've done was place a nice colorful Band-Aid over a gaping wound.

DADDY ISSUES

"Cent, come out here and meet your daddy." I ran out the house expecting to see Maurice White, the lead signer from *Earth Wind and Fire*. After all, my Mama said that that's who he resembled. Mama's been singing a tune all morning. She seemed to be in a good mood. It was a Saturday afternoon; she combed my hair and let me wear my "good" clothes. She wanted me to look my best for my very first visit with my dad. I was wearing one of my favorite outfits, tan knickerbockers with a matching gold stitched halter top, gold

Hercules sandals, and two tight pony tails in my head, hoping I was going to be cute enough for my daddy. Mama was looking quite snazzy herself; wearing a blue fitted flared bottom summer dress, flawless makeup and hair curls that looked light blonde clouds. The whole family was chilling out on the porch that afternoon during a hot summer day; Grandma, five aunts, three uncles and a few cousins. I think they were just as curious about him as I was. My younger aunts were always teasing me about my dad being a pimp, because his name was Jimmy "Mack" Nickolas. I heard through the grapevine that my mama got pregnant with me when she was 16. My grandmother didn't like my daddy because he was a grown man who had no business messing around with young girls.

Soon, a black *Cadillac* sedan pulled up in front of my grandmother's house with two gentlemen inside; the one on the passenger side was wearing a big black hat. My mom made her way to the car. She bent over to talk with the guy on the passenger side. My stomach started to flutter. I sat at the bottom of the porch steps, thinking, "What am I supposed to say to him?" I heard my grandmother and everyone else talking mad sh--- about my dad in the background. "Ole Mack Daddy, I see he still wearing that pimp hat," everyone laughed except for me. I was too nervous to think about anything else but his reaction to me. My mom looks back, soon she motioned for me to come to the car. I walk down to the front of the gate and stood there. I felt like I was being cooked by the sun with all that Vaseline on my face. I can feel the grass between my gold sandals. My mom called for me again, but for some reason,

I didn't move. I wanted him to get out of the car so I could get a good look at his face, check out what he was wearing, see how tall he was; I wanted him to pick me up in his arms. I wanted to know if my daddy truly looked like the dude from *Earth, Wind and Fire*. But daddy never get out the car. He motions for me to come closer. Still sitting in the car, "come here gal," he yelled. "Cent, that's your daddy girl, gone over there" somebody screamed from behind me. But I didn't move. I can't fully explain what I was thinking, or truly feeling that day, I was just six years old. I heard my momma saying to him, "why don't you just get out of the damn car?" He didn't listen to her. Instead, I remember him handing my mom a diamond earring, and before I could work up the nerves to approach the car, he drove off. It was my first, but soon realized it would be my last visit from daddy. Other than his name, which I'm not sure is real; I didn't know much about him. I tried searching for him several times, the only other information I knew was Daddy was a "rolling stone".

Hence, there are several other siblings that I have through him, whom I've never met. Oh, and that diamond earring, after my mom gave it to me, I dropped it in the grass as I watched him drive away. It was worthless, just as that visit made me feel that day.

For years, I was mad and blamed myself for not taking advantage of the opportunity to meet my dad and I often wondered why he never tried again. What was wrong with me, why didn't he want me? Was I just a mistake that he didn't want to be bothered with?

Over the years, I became quite uncomfortable with men. I struggled carrying a conversation or relating to men, I completely avoided being in their presence. This disposition carried over into my adulthood. I struggled with not knowing my father; longing for his involvement in my life during moments when I was being bullied or when I graduated from school. I'd look at myself in the mirror with many questions in mind: What features do I have of his? In what ways am I like him? What advice would he have given me, as his daughter? Often, I felt like I missed out on those things that only fathers can contribute to their daughters; attributes such as unconditional love, protection, provision and how to be strong, bold and confident. Maybe if my dad was around to tell me he loved me or that I was beautiful, I wouldn't have struggled so much with my self-esteem. My dad denied me of any rights to being a "daddy's girl". He wasn't available to give me away on my wedding day, to give his stamp of approval for any decisions I made in life. He denied his grandchildren any inheritance or legacy worth mentioning. I'm not sure if my daddy is still alive. But the older I get the less hope I have of ever meeting him again. I guess I will never get to be a "daddy's girl" and that's the fact of the matter!

UNCLE RICHARD

You know Uncle Richard, right? Every family has one! The uncle that lost his mind in the war, that friend of the family, the guy that loves to tickle the kids; especially those that were hungry for attention, like myself. It's that one uncle your mama warned you to stay away from. During a sleepover at a friend of my moms', Uncle Richard was up earlier than usual. He promised to watch cartoons with the kiddies in the morning. Most of the adults were still asleep. My mama was a snorer but somehow, she heard me giggling from the other room. "Cent, stop playing around, get in here and get ready so we can go. "Yes ma'am," I replied. The other kids had settled down but Uncle Richard wouldn't stop tickling me. "Give Uncle Richard a hug," he said. "Cent, what did I tell your ass?" said Mama. "Ok, here I come mama," I replied, as I stuck my thumb in my mouth. Uncle Richard, with a big smile on his face snatches my thumb out and rubs it between his hands "Bet you won't suck it no more" he said. I gave him an innocent punch to the stomach; surely, I wasn't going to put my thumb in my mouth after that! Immediately I rushed off to wash my thumb.

However, I didn't notice Uncle Richard was a few steps behind me. Before I knew it, he was shutting the door behind us. Still innocent, I say "Uncle Richie whatcha doing in here? I turn towards the sink and turn on the water. As the water ran; I felt myself being lifted from the floor. And now, I'm faced to face with Uncle Richard. I couldn't believe what was happening! He stuck his big wet tongue in my mouth. I could smell and taste the alcohol on his breath. He grabs my pocket book (my crotch), thoughts rushed through my head, "I don't like this tickle game, and "ewww his tongue is in my mouth?" This is wrong…I panicked then bit down as hard as I could. Instantly, he dropped me to the floor and kicked me on the side of my stomach as he rushes out of the bathroom. I sat there on the floor dazed and confused, as tears streamed down my face. "Mama gonna beat the black off me," I thought. "I can't tell her"! I wiped my tears, scrubbed my thumb and my tongue with soap, took a deep breath and walked calmly out, checking to see if anyone saw Uncle Richard leaving. Nope, no one noticed, thank God! Though discombobulated, I was relieved. But Mama had warned me about Uncle Richard, I guess I got what I deserved.

I was never quite the same after that experience. My innocence had been tainted. I didn't feel like a 7-year-old any more. I was shamed and felt dirty and ruined. I never told a soul about what happened; this was the onset of me becoming a silent sufferer. My encounter with Uncle Richard damaged any hope I had for having a healthy, trusting relationship with men. I didn't have a strong connection with my maternal uncles as they spent most of their lives in prison. With my Dad absence and now Uncle Richard's violation, my observation was right…men couldn't be trusted.

SCARLET LETTERS

Silent suffers are resilient and can bounce back from anything; we hear no evil, see no evil and talk no evil and can recover from most circumstances, so we think. I had withdrawn completely from men, including interactions with any of my mom's boyfriends and had disconnected from anything that would make my vulnerable (hanging around adults, being left alone with men, playing any kind of games that required touching etc.). I found a safe place in books and my Barbie dolls. Between the ages of 7-11, I lived in the public library; reading every fictional book I could find and embracing any non-fictional story in which I could relate. That was my past-time. The rest of those years were a blur. My pre-teen years were rough. As I loomed into puberty, my mocha complexion was over shadowed by acne and eczema. My naturally coiled pigtails that my aunt used to straighten on Sunday mornings, for Easter and picture day soon lost its shine and length to the over processing of boxed perms (which kept getting stronger with each touch-up). Soon enough, I had no hair. Everybody has at least one hideous childhood picture. It's that one picture that I would use as a target at the shooting range. Well, my target practice picture is the one from 5th grade school pictures. My mom made me wear this young dingy white laced church dress that I wore for Easter 2 years before. I could have chocked her when she purchased an 8X10 to hang on the living room wall! I hated that picture with a passion!!!! Sometime later, that photo magically disappeared.

Those adolescent years didn't spare me of any details of awkwardness. I was clumsy, shy, timid, afraid to talk, didn't want to be seen and hated drawing any attention to myself. I spent a lot of time fantasizing in the mirror, wishing I had lighter skin, slanted eyes, long hair, dimples; you know, all the physical characteristics that others found attractive. Instead, I was the bumpy face girl, the black ass girl, the dirty girl, the scary girl, the quiet girl, the dusty girl, the UGLY girl. The boys shunned me. Being isolated in such a way, I became the "invisible girl." One boy on the block made it his duty to call me ugly to my face every time he saw me and especially in front of a crowd of people. My friends and I would walk down Central Avenue on our way to the store and this guy would show up from out of nowhere, "Hey......so and so, hey this person, hey.... that person but to me, he would say, "Hey.... UGLY!" The boy called me ugly so much in one day that I began to answer to it. I didn't think to retaliate or stand up for myself; that would have made things worse. Instead, I subjected myself into a world of "insanity" I desperately wanted to belong so I did the same thing over and over expecting different results. I thought maybe, just maybe things will change. And when they didn't change, I made the adjustments. I tried my best to fit in, imitating others, wearing different hair styles, wearing make-up thinking this would improve my image. Nope, I was still ugly. I smiled and laughed at the jokes but my pillows told a different story. I recalled my first physical altercation; instigated by the neighborhood kids. The boys were relentless that day. The girls and I were playing double-dutch rope in the streets. I was up to turn the ropes when one of the boys threw a rock and hit me in the face. I was determined to stand up for myself that time! Holding back the tears welding up in my eyes, I dropped the rope and turned around to address whoever threw the rock. The girl that was jumping said that I hit her with the rope when I dropped it on the ground. "My bad," I said and carried on addressing the boy who was boasting about how he'd got me good.

Somehow, the girl and I got into this fight. She was a pretty big girl. I was scared and nervous that I could have peed my pants, but I had to do something; everyone was watching. She swung the first hit and our arms started swinging at each other like windmills. I got a few hits but man….. she tore me up! Before I knew it, she had me in a headlock and was beating on my head like a drum. The only way I could get her off was to bite her. I bit down on her arm as hard as I could. She loosened her grip and I dropped to the ground. My initial thought was to run. But as I was getting up, she grabs my spaghetti strap tank top from the back and pulled on it so hard that the straps broke and the shirt rips, exposing my breast. She finally let go! I quickly cover my chest with my arms. I cried loudly. I could hear everyone laughing and see them pointing their fingers. I took off running towards home, down the alley way, through the back door and up the stairs to my room. I slammed the bedroom door and fell onto my bed. I screamed in my pillow, "WHY????" I had no intentions of fighting that girl. "How in the world did that happen!" I was so embarrassed. Not only did I get beat up, but my little door knob breast was exposed for all to see. "I'm never gonna live this one down," I thought to myself. I wiped my tears, got up and walked over to the mirror. I would stare at my reflection, I thought, "YOU UGLY!" My hair was messy after having been pulled out of the ponytail. I was bleeding from the scratches on my face. I developed a knot on my forehead from the rock. My tank top was badly torn. I was a mess! I wanted to run away from home.

Then I thought, there's a better idea, "Why don't you just die! Yeah, kill yourself; silence everything and everyone around you!" I dashed into my mother's room, grabbed several pill bottles from her dresser. I ducked into the bathroom and emptied several pills from each bottle into one hand. I put the pill bottles back, snagged a cup of water from

45

the kitchen and went back to my room. Everybody was on the front porch enjoying the summer weather. "They didn't even notice me. I don't want to face those kids anymore, I'm tired of this and I bet I won't even be missed," I was convinced. I toss the pills in my mouth, gulp down some water and returned to my bed to die.

"Cent, Mama said get up and come go to the store," I could hear my little brother calling me in the distance. The sun is shined brightly on my face through the curtains; it had turned morning. "Cent, Cent" ...I heard in what seemed like a distance background as my brother banged forcefully on my bedroom door. I sat up in my bed in disbelief! "I'm still alive-this sucks!" I felt sick to my stomach. "Move," I pushed my brother to the side to make a fast break to the bathroom. The vomit barely made it in the toilet. "Mama wants you now," shouted my little brother. I told him to shut the hell up! "Oooh, I'm telling mama," he said, while running hurriedly down the stairs to Mama. After vomiting a few more times, I grab a towel to wash my face, rinsed my mouth out with water then looked up into the mirror, *"God, why did you choose me to be the ugly one. You hate me so much that you won't even let me die!"*

I continued to struggle with my identity and self-esteem through my young adulthood. I developed a false sense of confidence that initiated my engagement into some very unhealthy relationships. I started having sex at 14 years old and was pregnant by the time I turned 17. Becoming a mother made me realize that I had to change; otherwise my struggles could affect my child. Learning to love and appreciate oneself is not an easy task when dealing with a damaged self-image. When I looked in the mirror, I saw the reflection of a girl that lived in the shadows of others; a silent suffering, broken spirited little girl who was neglected and rejected by her father and peers. I had grown tired of her. Reading self-help books by prominent authors like Les Brown, Maya Angelou, Toni Morrison and Proverb 31 (Bible), helped me to find and embrace attributes and qualities that I overlooked. Because I had channeled myself to focus on the imperfections that I saw in mirror. This new-found appreciation facilitated my need and desire to be in relationship with God. I always believed He existed, I just didn't know how to get close to Him. My spiritual journey opened me to this revelation…. I've always been a "daddy's girl." God has been fathering me the whole time…protecting me, providing for my every need, keeping me safe from self-destructive activities and other demises that could have annihilated my existence. He gave me the strength and courage to endure those traumatic experiences so that I'd have a testimony and be a witness of his goodness & mercy. *Had I not gone through those experiences, I may not have come to a place of humility for God.*

Prayer for My Sisters
by
Cynthia Cherry

Father, I pray for all women that struggle with identity crisis, low self-esteem, low self-worth, self-doubt, and distorted images of themselves, those that are fatherless, feel ashamed, condemned, neglected, abused, misused and mishandled, and for those who may be suicidal, depressed, anxious, timid, shy and fearful. I pray for the brokenhearted, those who have been raped, are unforgiving, smitten and angry. I lift up those who are poor, feeble, down trotted, sick, disadvantaged, forgotten, lost and self-destructing. I cast down every vain and wicked imaginary thought that tries to exalt itself against the will, purpose and plan of God for their lives. Satan, I rebuke you, lose them now and take your hands off of God's property!

Father God, remind them that you are so mindful of them that you have numbered every hair on their head, that your thoughts of them is peace and not of evil to bring them to an expected end. That they are fearfully and wonderfully made and marvelous are your works. That they are unique, having been created in your image apart of your workmanship, designed for greatness

Arise O women of God and stand strong in the Lord and in the power of his might. You are loved, strong, courageous, beautiful, lovely, wealthy, prosperous, victorious, smart, innovative, creative, valuable and treasured by God. You are blessed and highly favored, more precious than gold, anointed and appointed. Do not bury your talents, your gifts…it was given to you by God for display of His greatness. He has given you power to create wealth. Let your oil flow, let your water refresh and let your salt be flavorful.

Arise O Virtuous Women of God and take your right place as royalty. Look in the mirror and fix your crown and glory, embrace and flaunt your phenomenal womanhood, motherhood, sisterhood, and livelihood so that that your light may shine, men will see your good works and glorify the name of our LORD.

Arise O Women of God and be Virtuous

About the Author

Cynthia Cherry, Co CEO of Alpha & Omega Transit Network Inc. a non-emergency transportation company has more than 18 years of experience in small business ownership and office management. Cynthia assisted in the establishment and operations of two small businesses, Cherry Property Management Inc. and Primerica Financial Services. As the co-owner of Cherry Property Management Inc., Cynthia was the Secretary and Office Manager; performing secretarial and clerical duties for four years. Cynthia joined Primerica Financial services in 2004 as an Independent Business Associate and provided financial services to families as a life insurance representative and office manager for 8 years.

Cynthia holds a Bachelor's of Science degree in Family and Consumer Science from Western Illinois University. Amongst her experiences as a small business owner, Cynthia possesses 20 years of early childhood education and social service experience. She has worked with children and families as a crisis interventionist, day care director, preschool teacher, case manager, adoption specialist, foster care licensing representative, parenting instructor and divorce/shared parenting seminar facilitator. In her nine years of employment with Webster Cantrell Hall Foster Care Program, Cynthia has been certified as a professional child welfare specialist, received certification to facilitate parenting classes, trans-parenting seminars and have been acknowledged for Exemplary Social Services to Children and Families and as Social Service Employee of the Year. In addition to being the Co CEO of Alpha & Omega, Cynthia currently holds the position as the Regional Training Manager in Central and Southern Illinois for Department of Children and Family Services Pride Foster Parent Training Program. Cynthia is a part of Community Love in Action, an outreach program that feeds the homeless in Decatur IL. She is a very active member in her church, Kingdom Come Ministry in Decatur IL; assisting in the administrative office and volunteering the community outreach program through Reasonable Service. Cynthia also works in youth ministry; teaching and assisting with vacation bible school and preschool bible study. She is a part of the ministry's leadership committee and a member of the choir.

LADY B SINGS THE BLUES
by
Barbara Cook-Strong

Life as a kid is supposed to be all good, but not when you have to move from your happy place in the hood. Changing everything you know, playing with who you know as friends on the block, kick soccer, *red light-green light* in the middle of the street. Fourth of July block parties with the families on the block…the fun, it couldn't be stopped! Then…BAM! We're moving to the south end of town that seemed so far away from the north end; what I knew as home, where I had so much fun, had true friends and a family unit. I don't want to start a new school or deal with new people. Will I even see anybody that looks like me? Having to change everything you know isn't what you imagined it to be, neither the truth nor the reality, of what you wished things would be.

Summer was over, and August was here. It was time to start the new school…huh! I'm no fool…this was not exciting to me as my parents tried to make it seem. As I began to feel stomach pain day after day. I cried and screamed, God please help me…take this pain from me! What was wrong with me as I keel over holding my stomach, as it rolled into knots. What is this from? Stress from the boys picking on me in class, hiding my desk in the closet, chasing me on the playground, pulling my hair because it was long and teasing me, telling me I wasn't better than the other black girls cause my hair is long! What damage kids can do and they think it's funny! My thoughts were...that wasn't funny, dummy! But thank God, he blessed me with a cousin who was a year older than me at the same school and I finally got enough nerve to tell him what was going on. Once, I did...need I say more, I didn't have to worry about those bully boys anymore! Who lived on the north end.... the place that I loved so much. All of a sudden, the south end didn't seem so bad after all.

This was my first step towards understanding diversity and other cultures with my new friend from Scotland. Until that one day my parents said we are getting a divorce! Anger and rage filled me. I was just plain mad, at the age of 12. You have got to be kidding me! I'm not hearing this, for what...why? I have only known us to be a happy family, always doing things together, family vacations, laughing, playing games in the back of my dad's Cadillac. What was I to do? I am the baby of the family, and my sister is almost six years older than me...her childhood is over. My home was divided, going this way and that way. I was lost and confused because I am a daddy's girl and there was no way I wanted to leave my father. I knew my sister would go with my mother, since I felt that she was her favorite; you know what I mean... just that feeling that kids get.

Facing a judge, having someone else other than your parents be a ruler of what you can and can't do. I vowed to never put myself in a place to be in front of another one to determine what happens to me in my life! Convincing this man that I didn't know and he didn't know me of how much I wanted to stay with my dad, in my home. All that I knew was my friends, and my school. My mind started racing and all types of questions began to formulate. Who is going to do my hair that stretches down my back? I am a girl, how can I ask my dad to buy me some tampons, let alone teach me how to use them. Finally, the day came when I had to go to the Judge's chambers and hope that he would let me stay with my dad. I didn't know what to expect, nonetheless, I thought the worse. However, when I arrived there, the office wasn't dark or cold; however, it felt big like it could swallow me up if I let it. Once the judge said you can stay with your father.... all that other stuff no longer mattered.

Life continued to keep moving full speed. Five years later and my mother finally won; I moved to California with my mom. I never intended to break my dad's heart, leaving him in Illinois separating an unbreakable bond. Who do I live for? This decision wasn't for me it was as if I was living to make one parent happy and to break the other's heart. My mother had remarried and yes, I had an attitude with this dude who thinks he's all that. "You ain't my daddy," was the thoughts that kept playing over and over in my head. I wanted to tell him that every chance I got, but I remembered my manners. I was raised to be respectful, so I did not say anything.

You know what we were taught; if you don't have anything nice to say, don't say anything at all! Well, this man who occasionally drank too much tried to make my life a living hell! Disrespecting me, calling me out my name and telling me I wasn't going to be shit. Really? I had a full-time job, going to college full time and a boyfriend. What else could he want me to do? It was as if he wanted me to be unhappy and miserable, but I was not going to give him that satisfaction. I was making it happen for myself! I hadn't planned on living on my own at the age of 18. Sometimes life situations can make you grow up faster than you had original planned. On top of that my best friend had moved from Illinois to California with me, and she had to endure this madness. I guess maybe that's why she stopped speaking to me and left California; or was it because she was mad at me, herself or her boyfriend? *What made her just pack up and leave without saying anything to me? I knew that whatever it was, I wasn't to blame, yet again losing something that I loved. Why are so many things I love being pulled away from me? God what are you telling me? Why don't I understand? Why can't you hear me?*

The love of my life was born the year of the new millennium, my niece, TT's little princess Alycia. This was a joy that I had never felt before. The feeling was amazing. I couldn't wait for the day for me to have a baby, especially if it feels like this. But God had a different plan that I wouldn't find out until years later. As I rushed from work in the middle of the day to meet my mother at my sister's house, because mothers have those connected feelings to their child especially when something doesn't feel right. Why hadn't my sister called us both as she normally did daily? Why wasn't my nephew at school and why hadn't my niece made it to the babysitter? Could the worst be in front of us? The answer was yes. As I looked up in the sky, all I could see were

54

helicopters. On the ground, yellow tape, onlookers, fire trucks, ambulances, and police were everywhere! Was this real? At that moment, I felt numb. The numbness became paralyzing as I made the phone calls to notify my family. My sister, my 15-year-old nephew were gone. My 22- month-old niece was shot, but survived! This part was a true miracle. The bullet was just 1 centimeter away from her heart. He eventually turned the gun on himself. There had been absolutely no history of domestic violence, y'all know, this was a total shock!

My body was numb, my mind was racing, and even though my feelings weak; I was filled with anger. I did not understand why this was brought upon us. What was to be learned from this? He answered quickly, "I am God and I saved her (my niece). In the midst of your storm I am here, lean on me and I will get you through this." I have always heard growing up in the church that God is a miracle worker. Even though you know that, I didn't fully understand that until we reached the hospital and the surgeon met us at the lobby and said, "I am finished with her surgery and she will have no problems recovering." Now you know that brought upon some great relief and true praise. In the middle of all this grief, you don't know which way to walk or which words to talk. I was speechless! Family, friends and people from everywhere came to be by our side. The love poured in. Stuffed animals and baby dolls were sent to show love and add a smile or two, to a baby who knew...that spoke to those who couldn't understand what she was trying to say. She was visited by little kids, moms and dads who saw the story on the news and couldn't go another day without coming to give their prayers and love. They asked to see her and cried and cried as their spirit died. Cry no more! Give God the Glory. The neighborhood kids held a candle light vigil and sang songs as they mourned and grew closer together. As a kid we fought, seemed almost like every day, but she was my sister and how dare you take her from me! I don't know if you can really hate someone that is dead...but I did. Is this what California had to offer me?

As if all this wasn't enough for one girl to endure, is there a cure? More tragedy occurred within my family. Not one, but two of my step-brothers gone! Back to back....one of a heart attack, the other of that monster called cancer. Feeling all alone, I went back home to Champaign to celebrate the life of my father at his Birthday bash. He too was a survivor as he was in remission from battling with his bout with cancer. At least I thought...his cancer had come back and the chemo treatments seemed to be even worse.

My visit was over, as he drove me to the airport to make my return to California, not only did I feel guilty for leaving him the first time and not pursuing my dreams; my soul was broken for letting him down. He became sick on the drive to the airport and as the pain built up in his stomach, I had to lay him down in the back seat of the truck as I thought whether to stay or do I go? This made me feel sick to my stomach. I decided to continue with my plans to return to California. How would I know that this would be the last time I would see him alive?

It was Easter Sunday morning and I was at home getting ready for church. My cousin calls letting me know he was at the hospital with my dad. Trying to hold it together, I ask my grandmother, what do you want to do as the doctor gave us a choice? While waiting for her to answer, I heard my father's voice saying, "I told you, I didn't want to be cut on again!" As we struggled to make a decision, he made it for us. Easter Sunday morning my hero died.

2002 through 2003 was a critical and mind blowing year for my family. All that happened would impact me for the rest of my life, positively and negatively. How do you get through the agony of losing so many of your immediate family within one year? Who do I live for now? How can I rebuild myself? These were the questions I asked myself as I looked over my life and focused on tools and books for healing. I read *Steve Harvey's Act Like a Lady, Think Like a Man, In the Meantime* by Iyanla Vanzant, *Copper Sun* by Sharon Draper, *Woman Thou Art Loosed* by Bishop T.D. Jakes, *The Coldest Winter Ever, Midnight and A Deeper Love Inside* by Sister Souljah, and the *Holy Bible*. Let the rehabilitation begin! Remodeling our family home, traveling, soul searching along with reading is what I did for the next year. During that time, I decided to make a difference in others' lives, to empower, to increase knowledge, and to give back to my community. I vowed to dedicate my life to help raise my niece. I would make sure she was loved unconditionally, supported and taught all the things that made me ambitious, strong, loyal, passionate and loving.

Life in the single lane being a TT/mom enjoying seeing her happy, playing with her cousins as I did back in the hood when nothing mattered, but fun. As I often thought, how would I help my mother get through her first born being taken? As I watched her hurt, I knew I had to change. First and foremost, I had to leave that stubbornness behind. As we worked together through this struggle we grew closer in a different way. Then I began to focus on my niece. I wondered, what questions my niece would ask as she got older. I prayed, "Oh God give me the wisdom to handle the coming days."

I imagined all of this that I had been through so early in my life was the reason why my hair shined like black coal with mixed sparkles of silver. I did not like my hair. At the age of 20, I believed I was too young to have grey hair. I dyed my hair on a regular basis for years to hide the silver; in which I found out was a symbol of wisdom. It took me a while to understand the beauty of premature grey (only my mother and her first cousin had this silver streak). But not before I heard remarks like "your face is young but your hair looks older, why do you have grey hair and you're young, are you the mother or grandmother?" Each time, the person I was with was much older than me. Really? God's word always prevails! At the age of 35, while in Chicago I met this older black lady who had beautiful grey hair. She told me, "baby your hair is beautiful, embrace it, and know that you are special and that people will wish their hair will grey like yours. God has blessed you to be unique and different. Stand out from the rest and no matter what, do not dye your hair anymore and embrace your blessing." That was the last time I dyed my hair. You know a good elders' wisdom when you hear it! I have loved my hair ever since and now see it is as part of my uniqueness. God turned the sour remarks made by those who tried to destroy my self-esteem into compliments. Haha!

Time kept on slipping…slipping…slipping in to the future. I know y'all remember this song.[4] As my time kept on slipping in to the future, I found myself into a twenty-year span dealing with dead end relationships after my first marriage. Conquering goals and wondering if I could ever see love again. Would I ever feel love again? This can't be possible for me, someone who understands the beauty of love and what it has to offer. Someone who didn't want to end up with a baby daddy…but instead with a husband and a family. I didn't want to end up revolving within a vicious cycle. What was wrong with me? That's all I could ask myself, as I found myself in front of the mirror more and more. Looking beyond skin deep and searching for the inner beauty but instead what I saw was this empty space and that God was telling me to be still and that there was nothing wrong with me! You know sometimes when you don't feel as valuable as you know you are or your self-worth has not been appreciated as it should have been? You begin to feel a certain way, questioning what you know is not the truth. God may be telling you too, to just be still; let me prepare you for a place that only I can take you as he continued to speak to me. The Church folk would say, "God told me this, God told me that," but as a child what does that mean? I had never heard God tell me anything and if he did I didn't know it was him. But at this point in my life it seemed as if I would spend the rest of my days alone, without meaningful

---

[4] These lyrics were written by Steve Miller and his band in 1977. The song is called *Fly Like an Eagle*.

companionship, someone to share my hopes and dreams, someone to love and cuddle with on those good ole couch days. Lord knows I didn't want that but if that was the hand I was dealt, then I was going to handle it as he designed it. I am far from perfect but I know I have a heart of gold and compassion towards others and I really thought that was enough. God will create a picture for you clear as day to bring you to new things.

As my journey continued, I traveled twice a year back and forth from Illinois to California to visit my mother and my niece after my father passed. Not knowing that on one of my visits after ten years that God would have me run into an old friend, whom I used to love to kick it with back in the day. He was true and dear to my heart. To see him again was wonderful, to get to know him again was exciting, and our dates were magical! At the end of my visit when I had to fly back home, I met him to say goodbye. Arms embraced with a kiss as soft as a whisper, my heart was beating fast as I turned to walk away. When I left him, I felt as if I left a part of my heart behind. But, I felt excited about this good feeling and asked myself could this be him, Lord? Married and divorced at an early age, did the possibility of love still exist for me? Is it possible to have love like I valued? Was this twenty-year journey of preparation for something or nothing? Well, guess what it was for something, my wonderful husband to be! For a time, you know with my luck, it couldn't be that easy. We endured a long-distance relationship. Yep, and guess what? When God has his hand in the mix all things are possible! As time lead up to this part, it was just what we needed, time to miss each other, time to talk day after day without face-to-face interruptions, the anticipation and excitement to see his face at the airport, was like the fireworks on the *Fourth of July*. Then our Caribbean vacation was it; he set it in stone for us to make that move towards spending the rest of our lives together. Finally, it was happening, but I still had that one problem lingering over my head. As, I mentioned earlier about me wanting to birth a child and God's plan was different; I fought fibroids for years and not being able to bear a child was crushing who I was as a woman. Love found me, but I still couldn't give birth. To have my man there supporting me as I lay there waiting for my surgery to begin, looking at the robot that would change my life, listening to the staff give me directions of what was happening next preparing me for the pain. What could they tell me to ease the pain in my heart? But God! Studies say that fibroids are a huge problem for women and it seems to be getting more severe; but this is how God works, in the midst of what we can't understand; God still blesses. He blessed me with a wonderful step-son and a beautiful step-daughter. One wise woman told me don't call them "step" and they won't act like it. Amen!   I was blessed with love…and he is my husband!

You see, life's journey will take us to places and spaces that we probably would have never imagined we would be; but no matter what road you take, keep God in the midst and let him be your high-beams when the road gets dark; when you feel as if you don't matter to people, or some person belittles you and tries to destroy your self-esteem. Know that you are a phenomenal woman and God isn't finished with you yet…as this should be…because we can never stop learning and empowering ourselves through his word and placing ourselves amongst positivity. Look in that mirror and begin to be true to yourself first. Understand all things about you and then work on those things that you need to change and focus on a healthy stronger you.

It's crazy because at an early age we start seeing a woman's worth destroyed by movies, lyrics and now social media...but they tend to lose focus that every boy and girl was born of a woman and how easy we forget their strength, power and value. Uphold yours! For me that strength came at different times of my life, each time I learned something new that I could continue to build a better me and then give that back to the community and through every organization I worked with. I surrounded myself with good people who have good spirits and those who love the Lord. Healing works best if it's simplified and staying away from negative people who mean you no good. Loving you is the most beautiful thing in the world, and remember God so loved the world that he gave his only begotten son. I have practiced thanking him for every lessoned learned that makes me stronger in my walk. I pray that whatever circumstances comes your way or whatever you have had to endure, that one of our stories encourages your fight to rise above and gives you strength to see all that is good. Stay inspired to increase your self-power and know that you can overcome all things through Christ that strengthens you. The phenomenal Maya Angelou once said, "I've learned that people will forget what you said, people will forget what you did, but people will never forget how you made them feel." The same thing goes for you.

I want to leave you with this scripture, Psalm 139: 13-19 says, "For you formed my inward parts; you knitted me together in my mother's womb. I praise you, for I am fearfully and wonderfully made. Wonderful are your works; my soul knows it very well. My frame was not hidden from you, when I was being made in secret, intricately woven in the depths of the earth. Your eyes saw my unformed substance; in your book were written, every one of them, the days that were formed for me, when yet there was none of them!"

Love and Blessing to you always!
Barbara Cook-Strong

About the Author

Barbara Cook-Strong is a passionate motivator for academic and social success and has been involved with organizations that are designed to create self-direction and professional development, such as Gamma Upsilon Psi Society, Operation Hope, Generation Next Leadership Academy, and The African-American Club.

Barbara continues to enhance student development while exercising her passion for providing academic advising, recruitment, and outreach to a diverse student population. As such, she has a flair for facilitating programs, workshops and special events for the benefit of helping others; as well as mentoring and bringing sight to unseen dreams. In 2014, she partnered with Dr. Tiffany Gholson on a project for rebranding the image of the black male youth with a video, "Suit and Tie in the 217", which decreased stereotypes and increased community awareness. She then created a Community March based on the 40 Days of non-violence movement with the Champaign-Urbana Black Greek Council and the Boy Scouts of America, who lead the March.

Faithful to her life of service, Barbara is the proud owner of *B. Strong Consultant Group*, an event planning and educational and career development program that offers support to young adults and continuing education learners with focus on motivation and guidance skills, development workshops, research, and marketing strategies.

Barbara received her Bachelor of Arts degree in General Studies from Eastern Illinois University and plans to continue her development by pursuing her Master of Arts degree in Educational Leadership or Counseling. She currently resides in Orange County, CA with her husband.

FREEDOM IN FORGIVENESS
by
Jataun J. Rollins

When someone shows you who they are believe them; the first time.
— Maya Angelou

When I look back over my life, I am thankful to God to be here in the flesh in my right mind, with a good measure of health------ and mostly whole. I studied nearly three decades of my journal entries to refresh my memory of events for development of this chapter.

It's a fact, God released me from several **bad** experiences, situations, decisions and relationships. Thankfully, I have evolved into the woman I have become today. In the past, I felt marked believing I was somehow to blame for the hurt I endured over the span of my life.

One early, resonant **UGLY** moment imprinted on my psyche was an event that occurred in early adulthood at about the age of 19 or 20. As a fatherless daughter, I was left to navigate and interpret without his guidance. I attended the annual *Taste of Chicago* summer food festival in downtown Chicago with my childhood bestie and her daughter.

The festival ended. We headed home towards the elevated train station, amid a massive crowd of people, in high spirits. My bestie and I reflected on our wonderful day together: people watching for several hours and sampling countless food vendors. Life was good! Lots of folk boarded the train and the train car filled quickly. It became packed with individuals of various ethnicities and mostly older adults. The joy filled day would soon be very short-lived.

Somehow, that day, I must have worn the "please f@#* up any type of joy that I'm feeling today" expression on my face. Out of nowhere an African American male in his mid-30s in the loudest voice he could muster began shouting in my direction. "DAMN, you got some big ass lips! I mean damn your lips are so big. How do you eat with them big ass lips?" Though his taunting lasted about 15 minutes, it felt like a lifetime! He didn't stop and I bowed my head and half-heartedly prayed for someone to speak up. I wanted so badly for someone to save me from that unwarranted public verbal whipping *Mr. Train Man* gave me. The train car was silent except for him while people just looked around as if nothing was happening. Maybe that is why, today, I am compelled to speak up in situations even when my safety might be at risk. Utter humiliation, is only an inkling of the damage that man inflicted upon me that day.

I repeatedly questioned myself in the moment and afterwards *Out of all the people on the train, why did he pick me? What look on my face did I carry that gave him consent to verbally assault me? What was it about how I carried myself that allowed him to think it was ok?*

66

He didn't know my story. He could not have possibly known that my lips were referred to as *soup coolers* or *Twizzlers* or *Mick Jagger's*. He didn't know I was bullied for nearly two years beginning in the 7th grade for being skinny, having a lisp with big teeth, big jaws, a gap in my teeth, big feet and later for wearing a jheri curl.

I'll take the hit for the jheri curl. To this day, I don't know what we were chasing when we he already had the curl pattern naturally. I digress.

Throughout that entire experience, my body was numb. I protected myself by envisioning I was having an out of body experience. I held my embarrassment like a big lump in my throat waiting to get air, so I can breathe because his words momentarily choked the breath and spirit out of me. Life had not prepared me for this. My parents had not prepared me for that day.

What should be noted is that my bestie was an African American, with naturally golden blonde hair, grayish green eyes and light skin. I walked in her shadow for years when we were younger because light skinned was in. I was used to fading to the back when a boy was seeking her attention because light skin wasn't in anymore and she relegated herself to the same position, fading to the back. I never thought less of myself though because of her looks. I just chalked it up to one's own personal preference.

Spike Lee's, *School Daze* raised social consciousness on the issue of color and I didn't see that hues mattered that much in my young adult days because I was comfortable in my own skin. I was in my element rocking Halle Berry's famous cut, short and tapered on the sides and back. I had a body to match without an ounce of cellulite or *love handles*. *Youthfulness* was on my side, but that day I felt different.

Once we de-boarded the train, my bestie and I never spoke of the *Train Man* incident as if nothing ever happened. I surmise it was just as painful for her as it was for me because we were like sisters. No words would have yielded any comfort to my self-esteem while at the same time the silence was deafening in not talking about it. It served as both my **healer and my torturer.** A pink elephant in the room trampling everything in its path. On one hand, I didn't want to discuss what happened to me, but on the other I yearned for my pain I experienced that day to be acknowledged.

As time passed I matured, I reflectively came to understand that the train incident occurred to help me get to the core of some unresolved issues I had stemming from what I thought was an irreparable relationship with my father and my desire for protection. That random stranger, Mr. Train Man, wielded an exorbitant amount of intentional energy to shatter my self-esteem. He was not my first bully, nor would he be the last.

I transitioned into young adulthood already scarred, carrying pain that I had pushed down out of consciousness., I would read a book later in life in about my thirties entitled, *Whatever Happened to Daddy's Little Girl?* that allowed me to process my life experiences as a woman without a father who navigated life with unresolved pain. That book helped me to gain an understanding of why I couldn't feel blissful happiness.

My father's absence, his inability to save himself from his own pain and his family, let alone me, established the lens through which I saw the world----- good or bad. Writing this chapter allowed me to make more connections with my lifetime of experiences of all the *"bads"* I spoke about earlier and the *UGLYs* I once carried with me.

I never shared this *Train Man* experience with my parents. That was a critical turning point in my life that not only provided a hard introduction to the cruelty of man, but highlighted how alone I felt having to bear that pain by myself.

Because of that day, *Mr. Train Man* changed my smile. I have always been complimented on my "Janet Jackson" smile that unbeknownst to folk was formed with intention to make my upper lip half its size to a thin lipped toothy smile. I learned how to camouflage the one of the biggest imperfections about myself. Beautiful on the outside and beat up on the inside. This "big lip" encounter ran contrary to the great part of my life as a young child growing up.

I lived in my grandmother's home within *Robert Taylor Homes*, the first four years of my life with both of my parents & my grandparents that bred a worldview of joy, possibilities, safety and infinite love. Yes, all that while living in the "projects." It was in that home I was provided with my foundation of learning and knowing the goodness of God, His grace and His mercy that was born in me to follow me all the days of my life.

As a very young child, my grandmother, Maggie Passmore, introduced me to religion, the "Pentecostal sanctified and filled with the holy ghost" kind. This began the formation of my relationship with God as I witnessed Grandma's devotion to the Lord. Grandma's life hung on this phrase to the time of her death, "If it's the Lord's will."

Although Robert Taylor was my first home, the wealth of my life experiences happened on the Southside of Chicago in a community called *Roseland*. My parents' work life afforded me a relatively beautiful childhood in a two-parent working class home sheltered from the bitter coldness of life from people like the *Train Man*.

I grew up in the 70s as a young, carefree black female child in a middle-class neighborhood albeit the leaner side of the middle class. All I knew is that we just lived. I didn't know what I didn't know. My upbringing was normal full of family gatherings, school and play. I grew up in a time when walking railroad tracks and through alleys were safe. I had plenty of neighborhood friends and didn't lack for anything. My mom had a *good* government job and my dad worked within the Chicago Public School system. We were you average black family.

Now let's get back to my journey from childhood to womanhood and how the *Mr. Train Man* incident intersects. I was admittedly a gangly, moderately chocolate, big teeth, fat cheeked awkward looking child. It cloaked me perfectly because I was oblivious to any feelings related to not being cute.

My father would walk through the house as long as I could remember, randomly doing this sing-songy thing in his booming voice, "Hazel Rollins ain't had no uuuugly kids and her kid's kiiiiids ain't had no ugly kids either!" I heard it enough throughout my formative years, I believed him because he was Papa and everything Papa said was "the truth."

I lived and breathed the "fairytale" where there was always a happy ending. The princess always found her prince charming, even from a frog with a kiss. Yes, I still hold on to the fairytale. I believe people are inherently good and I still believe that good things happen to good people regardless of life circumstances.

When I was twelve years old, my parents called my brother and I downstairs to the living room to ask us the million-dollar question. We stood side by side unsuspecting of how all of our lives were about to change. We mixed in with the chocolate brown shag carpeting, big oversized brown comfy couch, mirror tiled walls, colorful wheat grass plumes, white popcorn ceiling, wicker furniture and the big amber and green colored ashtrays.

I wondered what could they possibly have wanted, rousing me from my reading of George Orwell's book *1984*, one of the books my Papa gave me).

We could tell the tone of the moment was clearly a serious one in that my parents seemed to have had deep discussion about something that would have serious implications for the paths our lives.

The question came from my mother like she was asking do you want chicken wings or fish for dinner, "Do you want your Papa to leave or stay?" Slight Pause. Blank stare. Crickets. I spoke first, loudly, clearly and with the right amount of diction to let them know I meant it. "Yes, I want him to leave. He can go." My brother stood beside me with "crocodile tears" welling in his eyes at the tender age of eight, first trembling, then pleading "Papa, please. Please don't go Papa. Don't leave. Please Papa please." And then he sobbed; he had a bond with my father that was different than the one I had.

In that moment, I was not moved by my brother's tears or pleas and I didn't break because clearly, *he didn't know any better*. I think I was aware of my father's infidelity before my mother because Papa took me practically everywhere with him as a child. I was fed up and tired of sharing my father amidst two households. The other household of which contained my four-year-old brother by another mother.

I remember lying on the floor at about 3 or 4 years old watching Sunday *Family Classics* with Frazier Thomas on WGN recounting to my mom that Papa kissed a lady. I said it like it was nothing, I didn't know. I couldn't have known how hurtful that was for my mom to hear. I knew about that other relationship, I carried it with me for years. It took a toll on my mother's happiness and I felt we could do better.

So back to the big question my mom dropped on my brother and I in the living room and why I answered in the manner that I did. When I spoke loudly I spoke for me, my brother and my mother because somebody needed to do it. Fathers didn't openly live between two households nor did they allow drugs to consume their life, except it happened to us. It left a gaping wound that mostly all my sibs agree left an impact with exception of one.

I was selfish and didn't know the impact it would have on my brothers and my yet to be born sister. I just felt enough was enough and our family wasn't the same anymore. My thoughts, at the time, were my youngest brother was going to "reap the benefits" of a full time dad at his house because he and his siblings won, but my brother didn't---they didn't. Nobody won except the drugs. We all lost.

My father doted on me as a young child and I adored him too, but my father's addiction escalated and eradicated everything fatherly about him. Papa was the first man in my life to love and validate me. His departure could not have come at a more crucial time in my life, during pubescence, when I needed to understand the world around me and the changes that were happening within me. In the early 80s, crack cocaine devastated many families, unfortunately we were one of them.

I remember once, I intruded on my father as he was preparing to fire up a crack pipe He had moved back to our home, living in our basement. I asked, "Is there anything that can make you stop doing drugs Papa?" He looked me in my eyes with a cold look and clearly irritated that I was interrupting his flow and said, "No." What about your wife Papa?" He said, No!" Now I stood with crocodile tear rimmed eyes and a trembling voice. I asked, "Not even your kids Papa?" He stared at me with eyes bold, glaring and lips frayed back like the Joker from *Batman 3*, it was a side effect of the drugs. That was my way of knowing he had been using. Papa responded, "NO, THERE AIN'T NOTHING IN THIS WORLD THAT COULD MAKE ME STOP DOING DRUGS!" That was the day my father died on the very spot he stood because I couldn't understand his honesty in that moment which was the truth. Papa always told the truth. I wouldn't have a relationship with him for about another 15 years. He already missed 8th grade graduation, He would miss high school and then college too.

After my father's departure, his on again off again visits to the house were more painful reminders that we weren't whole. My mom was now a single mother for the first time in her life, married with three kids managing a home they bought together where she was to live out her happily ever after. Happily ever after never came.

So how do you bounce back from being a daddy's girl who adored and loved her father with everything in life to shift to the daughter who would utter the words "He can go?" I excelled in school throughout my academic career vying for the attention of my father to take notice that I was a "good kid" and the kids he had with my mom were not only good, but worthy of his love too. The only thing I had control over in my life was my grades, even when my world around me crumbled.

My family system rippled in waves of dysfunction and I often yelled through the house during adolescence reminding anybody listening how dysfunctional we had become. This is still a sore spot for my mom as she vividly recalls my outbursts from time to time now in more of a joking tone, but back then there was no humor in my perceived reality.

Life went on without Papa and my mom did the best she could with what she had to make sure we were okay. She struggled to make sure his absence didn't have an impact on us being successful in life. Eventually, I grew into my own rhythm dropped the tom boy persona and cute for sexy and sultry. The days of fighting boys were over. I didn't jump fences or out of trees anymore. I was a maturing woman with no anchor; the two-parent foundation I had was gone. I was a female without a father figure which proved to be a detrimental lapse of guidance in my life that left me empty.

Imagine a bottomless vessel despite how much you pour in, it cannot be filled. My relationships were matchless to resolve my emptiness. Who knew how impactful his addiction and departure from the family would have an indelible imprint on all our lives.

My father was not present to provide the affirmation, wisdom, guidance and love that I needed from the male perspective. My father was still dead to me, and I grew to be more damaged and learned unhealthy coping skills to deal with his absence until I demanded more of myself.

I yearned for a better, more purposeful life. I drew from my roots and reconnected with the church and learned forgiveness. I had to forgive myself, forgive others and most importantly forgive my father because it was not until then that I could be freed from the bondage of my past to move forward. I carried the weight of his life decisions from my childhood to adulthood that wasn't mine to bear.

At 21-years-old I birthed a beautiful, doe eyed daughter, the color of frothy cappuccino whom I named Joélle. I knew parenting was a serious responsibility. The life I planned for my daughter was to have a two-parent household and for her to be much more whole than I. I didn't want to inherit any of my *UGLY* ways: having a pattern of choosing broken men, seeking validation from men, feeling lost and disconnected or being self-conscious about looks.

Church found me again and it was my weekly refuge, from my complicated life, that filled me up enough to get to the next Sunday. I shielded Joélle from as much as *UGLY* as I could as she was without a father. My belief was that with a spiritual foundation she would never part from it. I embraced the preacher's messages and began to apply the principles of the bible to my everyday life, mainly ***forgiveness***. Faithfully, we attended for a year awaiting my moment to walk down the aisle to take the right hand of fellowship. The sermon that moved me was filled with metaphorical language about the game of chess that enabled me to believe the game of life was not over. I was just beginning with my faith walk with Christ. I found myself gliding down the aisle towards Reverend Dr. Jeremiah A. Wright who sparked a fire in me, helping to repair my spirit and allowing me to embrace being 'Unapologetically Black and Unashamedly Christian." My daughter was in tow gliding right with me in August 1996. We were both baptized together in April 1997 with my then fiancé who came into my life the year prior. God took away my spirit of cussing, granted me the desire to be in relationship and opened my heart to love. Love found me again y'all!

My new walk with Christ coincided with the timing of my new relationship with my fiancé, a former sweetheart & friend, who was about to engage me in a battle of a different kind that I had not ever experienced before. We never got to avow our love through sickness and health, for richer and for poorer and all the days of our lives.

One day, my reason for breathing was at the bottom of the steps and my former love and I were engaged in an argument that roared and echoed through the thin walls of my home and he grabbed me by both arms with a quick jerk. I had another out of body experience, the made for Lifetime Channel kinda stuff and could not believe this was happening to me.

My *UGLY* grabbed me and threatened to throw me down the stairs when my eyes met my six-year-old daughter with tears streaming from her face with a look of horror in a moment suspended in time. Her blood curdling scream rang like an alarm unlike anything I have ever heard in life. That day was the day I regained control over my life and I ended out engagement two months before the wedding. I decided to "save face" then rather than later deal with a messy divorce and create more heartache. I wondered if my father would have been the man he first presented to me from birth if I would have had to take that journey.

At the ripe young age of 46, I have experienced many disappointments, failed relationships & setbacks, but unrelentingly I have hung on to "joy coming in the morning." My father and I are the best of friends and he has been free from addition for over thirteen years. We picked up where we left off in the best of my childhood. He and my mother are good friends as well and support one another, especially when it comes to their children.

My faith in God prevailed once I understood how genuine I needed to be with myself first, recognize what I needed most. I searched for it and chased it down until I got it and I don't intend to let go. God has blessed me to experience love, show love, receive love, and know love since those earlier periods in my life so now I experience love with all my senses. Love rested on everything to get me through the lowest of valleys in order for me to walk in the clouds and shout how good God has been to me. I pray you know love too and hold to God's undying love for you.

About the Author

Jataun J. Rollins, AM, LCSW is a mother of two children, an aspiring author, therapist and an administrator in child welfare for over twenty years advocating on behalf of children and families. The expanse of her experience includes group sessions with nonresident fathers to overcome barriers to engagement with their children; providing families with resources to aid them in caring for their loved ones who live with Alzheimer's and other dementias; educating undergraduate graduate students in schools of social work; facilitation of supervision and test preparation for more social workers to acquire their license and speaking publicly on a myriad of topics at the national, regional and local level.

Ms. Rollins found joy in being a caretaker for her maternal grandmother, Maggie Passmore, for several years and a respite provider for her grandfather, Booker T. Passmore, and extended family which was just as gratifying. She plans to publish a memoir of experiences in which she utilized humor and relied on the faith her grandmother embedded in her earlier on that everything in life is according to "the Lord's will." She is committed to sharing her family's story to give hope to the masses of caretakers who struggle daily to wake up on the right side of the bed when the wrong side can't be an option.

Ms. Rollins graduated with a bachelor's degree in Psychology from Eureka College and a master's degree in Social Work from University of Chicago SSA. She enjoys connecting families to their roots via genealogy research, traveling and spending time with extended family. She has a private practice in the south suburbs of Chicago where she resides.

6

BEAUTY & THE BEHOLDER

by

Genesis A. Hall

"The common eye sees only the outside of things, and judges by that, but the seeing eye pierces through and reads the heart and the soul, finding there capacities which outside didn't indicate or promise, and which the other kind couldn't detect.[5]" – Mark Twain

"**B**eauty is in the eye of the beholder..." is a term that has been utilized over the years to essentially mean that everyone holds a different perception of beauty. Individuals ideology of beauty and their preference change like the wind. So why do we put so much confidence in what others view as beautiful? Why do we hold so dearly to another person's perception of what they believe as "UGLY" and allow this to shift our perception of ourselves?

Many of us are haunted by negative phrases that have been spoken into our lives and rejection we received from others. Many of us allow past traumas to dictate who we are, or we fight to seek the approval of man, and their definition of who we should be. Oft times, we walk around with an

---

[5] Mark Twain's *Personal Recollections of Joan of Arc-Chapter 11* entitled *The War March Is Begun.* http://www.online-literature.com/twain/recollections-joan-of-arc/19/. Retrieved March 7, 2017.

invisible tape and continuously replay self-depreciating phrases that cripple us from succeeding in relationships, in our careers, and in life generally. But this was never what our Heavenly Father willed for us to endure. However, this was the reality of my life, for countless years.

After years of peeling layers for self-discovery and searching for purpose as well as meaning, I noticed lying deep inside a negative tape that was fed by circumstances that I faced in my life. The circumstances included the *inconsistency of my father in my life, the emotional absence of my mother, molestation by a female, molestation by an older male in the church, molestation by family members, molestation by a boyfriend of my mother, rape, hurts in romantic relationships, and hurts in friendship relationships.* The two negative phrases deeply rooted inside were: "You are not enough" and "You don't matter!" This negative tape silenced my voice, crippled my esteem, and left me feeling rejected to the point of not desiring to live. "The world would be a better place if Genesis didn't exist", I thought. Although I could intellectually identify this as a lie, my soul was bruised by negative experiences in life that fed into the negative tape and led to low self-worth. Depression, anxiety, and approval seeking became a norm. Until **TRUTH** came in to silence every lie that circumstances, past hurts, and relational difficulties tried to speak in my life.

At a very young age, I was taken advantage of by an older girl and was molested while in the first grade. It appeared that there was a marker on me that said "violate me." Years later I was molested by two family members, an older boy in "the church", and one of my mother's boyfriends. In addition, in my early teen years my virginity

82

was taken by way of a rape. "So surely there must be something wrong with me," was the ever-present thought that played in my mind. My dad was not consistently in my life, hence, the idea of being protected was far from my understanding. Due to her drug addiction, my mother was emotionally absent. During that time, she became involved in several dead end romantic relationships. The idea that I didn't matter was planted and its roots deepened when my mother chose to remain in a relationship with one of her boyfriends who molested me.

Soon, I began to believe my life didn't matter. I repeatedly thought, "I must not be worth saving or protecting." My voice appeared to be silenced and I sought attention in attempts to "matter" to others. My worth hinged upon approval and acceptance from others. I attempted to seek approval from peers. Those peers would degrade me because of the length of my hair and thickness in my thighs. These names were often hurled at me: *Baldhead, Fat cheeseburger,* and *Ham hock thighs.* These nicknames began to shape the definition on what was believed to be undesirable or *ugly*.

As early as the first grade, I constantly compared myself to my peers. I was not enough. My hair wasn't long enough. I wasn't thin enough. My smile wasn't enough. I wasn't good enough. My reality of beauty had been tainted. Soon, I turned to food and begin to involve myself in promiscuous relationships in my early teens to mask the hurt that laid deep inside. I wanted to fill the pain and not allow myself to feel the pain. I desperately desired to feel wanted and accepted. However, I was constantly faced with challenges that fed the lies that I was not enough or I did not matter. I sought romantic relationships with individuals who I believed would protect me or accept me. However, I often was left used and thrown to the side. Eventually, a deep anger rose on the inside of me. I began to erect a wall to protect myself. I developed ways to attempt to hide the hurt but heartaches, failures, and setbacks seemed to agitate the deeply rooted seeds of pain. The hurt began to seep out in various ways. Withdrawal, blow-ups, tearfulness when corrected, and completely breaking down, served notice that something on the inside of me was corroding my confidence and esteem. I transferred my energy to attempts to be perfect but noticed that perfectionism caused me to internally beat myself up because nothing was "good enough" echoed in my soul. This caused me to retreat and not take risks because of fear of failure.

By the time I reached college, things began to change. My spiritual relationship with God began to deepen. I always attended church as a young girl, and even went alone. I knew how to attend church services, sing songs of praise, and read scriptures but I did not know how to love God or surrender my heart totally to Him. I was privy to religion, but still needed to understand how to build a relationship with God. I couldn't trust Him. I couldn't trust anyone. Past hurts and feelings of abandonment gripped my soul and effected my ability to fully receive the merciful love of Father God.

During college, I found myself alone away from family and friends. It was in this alone time I clung deeper to God and began to attend a ministry that focused on the power of God. I learned that God was living, He heard me, and He

84

spoke. I learned the power of prayer as a way for me to communicate with my Creator. I learned to quiet myself to hear His voice. I began to spend more time in prayer and advance in my revelation of the power of the Holy Spirit. And I learned more about His ability to heal, deliver, and set me free.

The more I prayed the closer I felt to God. The closer I felt to God the more I learned about my identity. Although I had a difficult time seeing God as my strong tower and protector due to the hurt, it was as if He performed surgery on me and gave me a new heart. The surgery was precipitated by me asking God to show me how to love. I desperately needed to be set free from the cage of isolation and the self-defeating thought processes of not being "enough or mattering". **Forgiveness was the gateway to my freedom.** I discovered this was necessary in my quiet time with the Lord. As He began to search my heart and unveil the deep hurt and severe wounds, I immediately began to understand how my growth was stunted. It became significant for me to forgive God, to forgive myself, and the countless others who had betrayed and violated me.

I'm not certain of *UGLY* issues you faced in your life, but if you need to forgive yourself and others, I want to share with you three tools I consistently used to become free. They are as follows:

1. ***Journaling***: I began to journal my feelings and hurts. I was honest about how I felt. I took time to outline the negative and positive things that happened in my life. I also identified what I learned as TRUTH versus

the lies in my life. I identified scriptures and *I AM* statements within my journal writings. I rehearsed these scriptures and affirmations. For example, I rehearsed the following: "I am not abandoned. My God is with me, in me, for me, and goes before me." Deuteronomy 31:8 became a staple. It reads: "The Lord himself goes before you and will be with you; he will never leave you nor forsake you. Do not be afraid; do not be discouraged." Any time past events would attempt to stifle me and become triggers, or when subtle lies attempted to creep in, I would use this and other scriptures to shut it down. The TRUTH of God's word and affirmations gave me life.

2. ***Writing letters***: I wrote letters to God, myself, my mother, and others. The letters focused on past hurts, and my decision to move forward and forgive. I also wrote an apology letter. I apologized for the residual effect of not forgiving. Harboring hurts and not forgiving impacted my relationship with God, myself, and others (my mother). I provided my mother with a letter which opened the door for her to respond. In that letter, she revealed how she too suffered from past hurts, which in turn crippled her response, and developed in her the inability to nurture or protect me during my molestation. This was huge for me! It helped strengthen our communication. It tore down the walls I built to keep her and others out.

3. ***Thanksgiving, Prayer, and Blessings***: I used prayer
   and thanksgiving to heal, which led me to bless those
   who hurt me. I thanked God for who He originally
   created them to be. I consistently prayed for
   forgiveness and repented for my actions such as the
   inability to forgive, to be honest, for offending them,
   for my unresolved anger, and unhealed hurt. I spoke
   blessings instead of curses upon them and released
   them to God.

The healing began when I first addressed my relationship
with God. I honestly expressed to God those raw feelings of
worthlessness. Soon God helped me understand that it was
never in His plan for me to be hurt or abused. God showed
me that He was with me all along, protecting my mind and
reminding me of my value. Matthew 10:28a and verse 31 in
the Amplified version, says "Do not be afraid of those who
kill the body but cannot kill the soul...So do not fear; you are
more valuable than many sparrows." I want you to know
YOU too are MORE VALUABLE than sparrows! WE ARE
MORE VALUABLE than sparrows!

The Lord began to show me that Jesus Christ was
beaten, bruised, and hung on the cross for my sins,
transgressions, iniquity, grief, shame, trauma, and past hurts.
He reminded me that *hang-ups* in life happen but that Jesus
hung the hang-ups on the cross and left them there so I did
not have to bear those burdens in my own life. This enabled
me to truly begin to live an abundant and free life!!! The love
of ABBA Father through the death burial and resurrection of
Jesus Christ, helped me to know that no matter what

happens, my heavenly Father loved me, loves me, and will continue to love me. His love for me was never predicated upon me being perfect. He helped me to know that I always mattered to Him and was perfect in His sight. I mattered to Him so much that He allowed His *only* begotten Son Jesus Christ to die on the cross for my sin and rise with all power in His hands. He reminded me that He loved me so much that He did not leave me or forsake me! Hebrew 13:5b-6 Amplified versions says, "I WILL NEVER [under any circumstances] DESERT YOU [nor give you up nor leave you without support, nor will I in any degree leave you helpless], NOR WILL I FORSAKE or LET YOU DOWN or RELAX MY HOLD ON YOU [assuredly not]! So, take comfort and become encouraged and confidently say, "THE LORD IS MY HELPER [in time of need], I WILL NOT BE AFRAID. WHAT WILL MAN DO TO ME?'"

God loves me (and you) so much that He didn't leave me comfortless but He gave me the Helper the *Holy Spirit*. John 14:16 Amplified reads, "And I will ask the Father, and He will give you another Helper (Comforter, Advocate, Intercessor – Counselor, Strengthener, Standby) to be with you forever." It was by way of the Holy Spirit, that my identity began to unfold. I was not my past or my circumstances but I was the blessed beloved daughter of the Most High God (Genesis 1:28). I am created in the image and likeness of my Creator (Genesis 1:28). My Heavenly Father in the beginning of time created me very good (Genesis 1:31). My Beauty was in the eye of my beholder…my God, not man!

Because of this revelation, God took me through a process of forgiving myself and forgiving others. He began to restore my voice, as for years I remained silent. This silence was eating at me internally and externally it began to show in my weight gain. At one point, I weighed nearly 300 pounds. During this time, I began to question God about his ability to deliver me from things such as fornication and cursing, but my physical body had yet to experience this freedom. He had assisted me in overcoming some of the most challenging times of my life. I remember studying for my Master's Degree in Social Work and maintaining my sanity, this was only an act of God! However, overeating and finding the strength to exercise was another story.

Soon, God revealed that there was more I needed to release, and there was more TRUTH I needed to let in.
He showed me that I needed to let go of the "weight and sin" that easily beset me (Hebrew 12:1). I did not realize that for years, I did not look at myself in the mirror. I did not like what was staring back at me. The taunts of the negative tape of not being enough started to speak louder than the TRUTH that was revealed. So, finally, I cried out to God, "show me…. me the way you see me!" And He did! He began to reveal to me a picture of this thinner version of myself amid the larger me. During that time, I finally would glance at myself in the mirror. Beauty would radiate back at me. God saw something beautiful in me at a size 26, and finally, that beauty became visible to me. I began to believe what God said about me. I started to behold the beauty of *my* beholder.

Eventually, years of unraveling lies and releasing forgiveness, began to show in my physical body. I had to love myself, all of me. At nearly 300 pounds, I began to rehearse the Word of God over my mind and body as I walked around in my home. Soon, I gained confidence and started walking outside, then I joined a local gym. As I was releasing hurt and gaining confidence, I was shedding pounds *supernaturally*. I lost nearly 120 pounds![6]

As I was shedding pounds, I began to gain confidence which allowed me to regain my voice. I became more open and honest about the impact of past hurts. I started setting boundaries in relationships. I was easily able to forgive. My walls began to come down and I could love freely again. This new-found freedom helped to restore my relationship with my mother who I once was unable to say I loved but now she has become my biggest cheerleader and I love her dearly! I could open my heart to love without the fear that someone would hurt or misuse me. I am now able to use my story for God's glory and help others who experienced past trauma. This gave me the confidence I needed to support others in my private practice as a Licensed Clinical Social Worker. I can effectively enlighten, inspire, encourage, and impact lives for the purpose of soul prosperity (3 John 1:2). My mission is to empower others so they are liberated from debilitating thought patterns and pains from their past. The very thing the enemy tried to destroy me with became a stepping stone to help bring freedom to others. For this, I am eternally grateful! Today I learned that my beauty, my worth, and the

---

[6] More of the 7 year process of my weight loss can be read in my upcoming book, *Supernatural Weight Loss*.

essence of who I am does not lie in the taunts from others, the trauma of my past, and the hurts in my life. My beauty and worth is defined by my Heavenly Father who accepted me as His own because of the finished work of Jesus Christ. He never abandoned me and never will! I have this evidence with the power of the Holy Spirit, the Spirit of Truth, who speaks loudly, silencing every lie and eradicating every unrighteous thought pattern. I am whole! My beauty is in the eye of My Beholder…My God!

Ultimately, it's important to know *and* believe. In my time of reflection, the Holy Spirit revealed that knowing is the ability to internally have awareness of somethings existence. However, believing is the ability to internally understand in your heart and hold this as the absolute truth! Today, I know I am beautiful. I believe I am beautiful. Now, I want you and countless others to come to this same TRUTH about yourselves as well, and affirm this TRUTH within.

About the Author

Genesis Hall, LCSW is a visionary, motivator, intercessor, teacher, helper, counselor and compassionate child of the Most High God and is now on a mission to enlighten, inspire, and impact for the purpose of soul prosperity. Cleaving to the blessing given in 3 John 1:2, which says "Beloved, I pray that in every way you may succeed and prosper and be in good health [physically], just as [I know] your soul prospers [spiritually]", Genesis is pioneering a movement of self-discovery, self- acceptance, and fitness through her Supernatural Weight Loss Support Group. After losing nearly 120 pounds, Genesis uses her testimony, experience, and support group as an avenue to encourage others by providing accountability, encouragement, and sustainability in the weight loss journey utilizing spiritual principles to generate effective life changing results through the power of God.

Genesis is a licensed clinical social worker who provides individual and family counseling services to children and adults in her private practice in Central Illinois. Genesis graduated from Illinois State University with a Bachelor of Science Degree in Sociology in 2002 and obtained a Master of Social Work degree in 2005. She has used her education to dedicate over thirteen years in the field of social services to individuals with behavioral and emotional disorders in Central Illinois. God has gifted Genesis to reach out to the hurt and vulnerable and she has a heart to use her God given talents to help minister healing to the hurting and transform lives. Genesis combines her faith and education to fuel her vision of helping others become healthy, physically and spiritually by hosting speaking engagements, seminars, and facilitating trauma trainings.

Genesis began her life in the inner city of Chicago, IL and currently lives in Bloomington, IL. After facing some of life's toughest challenges, Genesis can testify of Gods saving grace through Jesus Christ. Genesis serves at House of Faith International Christian Church in Bloomington, IL, under the leadership of Pastor T.D. Brewer, on the Praise and Worship Team and in the Helps Ministry. She lives a lifestyle of prayer, praise, and worship to her heavenly Father.

7

IT'S BETTER TO MARRY THAN TO BURN
by
SHERRI HAMPTON

Some things are kept or meant to be kept unknown or unseen by others. Fear is meant to paralyze you and render you motionless. As a child, because of my fear, I made the decision to keep a secret and never tell a soul, especially my parents. They never knew that their only daughter had been molested. How do you tell mommy and daddy that their little girl's innocence has been taken away? I was supposed to be playing with dolls and baking cakes in my *Easy Bake Oven.* I played with lightening bugs and climbed trees. I wasn't supposed to be learning how to hide pain behind my giggles and my eyes, but I did. I did not fully understand why this was happening to me, but I did know that this was too much hurt and pain for a child to keep inside.

Some memories are so painful that we find various ways to deal with them. I suppressed being molested so deep within myself, it was as if the act became unconscious to me and it remained that way for many years. I went on with life, giggling, playing with my friends, and going to school like nothing happened. I was active in school, I ran track and tried my hand at basketball. I was a pretty normal kid. I remember out of nowhere I started to have visions of my childhood, also known as flashbacks. I would see vividly the faces of people I knew, and places that I had been and I had no idea what I was remembering. I did not want to say anything to anyone about what I was experiencing, as I was still unsure myself. Initially I thought it had to be dream. I did not understand where these memories were coming from and what they meant. I was not sure what triggered these feelings and made them resurface. However, I soon started to put it together. I would continue to hold on to my secret, I would not tell. I was more worried about how everyone else would feel, and perceive me. I put my feelings and needs aside and went on with my life. Honestly, I did not think that after all these years anyone would believe me anyway. Maybe they would think that I was making it up. So, I did like a lot of girls and boys do, I continued to suffer in silence, alone. I just wasn't ready to talk about it with anyone. I would go on with my life as a normal teenager. I went to dances, football games, and hung out with my friends. I had a few boyfriends during my high school years, but it would be the one I met when I was 15 years old, that would change the course of my life forever.

I remember so clearly my grandfather's voice saying that the bible teaches that, "it's better to marry than to burn." Shacking up, or living with a man which is also known as living in sin, was not an option for me. My grandfather was an old-fashioned Baptist preacher that I have fond memories of growing up. He believed that women should not wear pants in the sanctuary, or preach in the pulpit. He was the beloved pastor and founder of our church for 37 years until he passed away in 2006. My grandfather married three times and I would follow in his footsteps, and would marry 3 times as well.

My parents were married for 18 years. They were far from perfect, but they worked hard, and provided my brothers and I with the best life they knew how. I was the oldest of three. I was 2 years older than my middle brother and 7 years separated the youngest and I. I remember many happy times growing up. We took family vacations every few years, and my parents made sure we had all that we needed, and some of our wants. My parents married very young; my mom was still in high school when she had me. My dad would go off to the Army, and my mom and I went with him. I don't have any memory of that period. Flash forward a few years, I remember my parents would hang out with their friends, most of them were other married couples. They would host card parties at each other homes and play music and have a good time. They all had kids and back in the day parents took the kids to the party too. No matter what happened on the weekend, my mother made sure we went to church every Sunday and she went with us. My mom was in the choir and although dad drove the church van he very seldom went to church. I was young but I knew that there were troubles in their marriage. I would hear the late-night arguments when they thought we were asleep. I do not know all that my parents went through in those 18 years, but I do know they loved us and gave us a good foundation for life. I believe my parents stayed together for as long as they did to raise us. I don't doubt they loved each other, I just believed some of the things they went through were hard for them to recover from. My parents separated shortly after my 19th birthday and divorced soon thereafter. One of my brothers went to the Air Force shortly after graduating. My baby brother was still in grade school, he and my mother moved out into their own house. I did not go off to college like my friends; I stayed and began my trilogy of marriages.

It's better to marry than to burn. I remember I couldn't wait for Sundays and the skating rink. My girlfriends and I had on our matching shirts and starched jeans, and we were talking about all the cute boys we'd see there. It was the highlight of every week. I was a little shy and didn't really know how to talk to boys. There was one that I could not wait to see every Sunday. He was tall, good-looking and I would watch him skate. Once, I got up the nerve to ask a mutual friend to introduce us we hit it off almost instantly. I was a sophomore and he a senior. We dated all through my high school years. We were stuck together like glue for the next few years. I honestly don't remember him asking me to marry him, I think it was just a mutual decision we made without a lot of thought. I believe that it was just expected because we had been together for so long. We just started telling our families that we were getting married and started planning. I was 19 years old and he was 21 years old when we tied the knot. I was a wife now, and had no clue what that really meant. We were still trying to figure out who we were as individuals. We settled into a tiny one bedroom apartment that we fixed up and made our own. It felt like we were playing house in the beginning. It was good for the first few months, and for the most part life was routine. We spent time

96

with family and friends, went to work and did regular everyday stuff. I really do not know what if anything really happened but our relationship started to change. I started walking on pins and needles feeling very unsure about what was going on. He became distant and our relationship was tumultuous to say the least. We went on like that for a few years arguing, fighting, and making up. I remember being sick for a while, thinking I had the flu. It went on for a few weeks, so I decided to go to the doctor. To my surprise, I was 6 weeks pregnant and what I was experiencing was morning sickness. We never talked about starting a family, but here I was pregnant. I remember the overwhelming feeling of fear and happiness I felt. I was going to be a mommy! He was excited too. The next 7 months went by rather quickly. The turmoil eased up a bit during my pregnancy, as we prepared for our little princess. She was so beautiful and we were so happy to welcome her into our lives. Being a mommy was such a joy and there was nothing else in my life to compare it to. We were both so in love with our little girl.

We spoiled her rotten. She was the glue that held us together. We would go on to purchase our first home and tried to make it work for our family. We experienced highs and lows during our marriage and I honestly think we tried the best way we knew how, but we soon came to the end of the road. I was heartbroken that my marriage was coming to an end after only 5 years. We had been together since we were teenagers, we practically grew up together. However, I knew it was for the best, but it was so hard to walk away. To be honest, I probably would not have ended it on my own. I probably would have stayed and just dealt with it. I remember my husband saying, "we deserved to be happy". I was scared and felt all alone, as this would be the first time I lived on my own. I now had a 3-year-old daughter that was counting on me to be her mommy, and to love and protect her. I had to be strong for her, no matter how much I was hurting on the inside. I felt like a failure. I would go on though and take care of my daughter with the help of her dad and our family. I adjusted to being a single parent, I worked every day and eventually started going out with friends and dating. I had a few relationships over the next few years but nothing ever lasted long. I really didn't like being single and longed to be in a happy successful relationship, and eventually get married again one day.

It's better to marry than to burn. He walked into my job one day, and I remember thinking to myself, "I've never seen him before." The attraction was mutual. We exchanged numbers and it was not long before we were dating. I must admit there were numerous red flags in the beginning, but I chose to ignore all of them. I saw potential in him, but I honestly don't think he saw it in himself. We dated briefly, and moved in together within a few months. He had been lying about his living arrangements; his significant other had put him out after she found out about me. I felt bad that he had no place to go, instead of being upset about being lied to. He was very unstable when it came to keeping a job, and was unemployed a lot. We would get together with friends play cards and cook out all the time. I was starting to fall in love again. I knew we had issues and my woman's intuition was on point when it came to him. I should have known that he would cheat on me because he did it to his previous girlfriend with me. I really should have walked away right then. I chose to stay and it got worse. I learned he was having a baby with another woman. The news of this devastated me. I was distraught that he had been cheating, but worse than that, I found out I too was pregnant. I was extremely ill as I experienced morning sickness for fourteen consecutive days.

Things went from bad to worse. Soon, I decided that I could not continue with this pregnancy. I made the decision to terminate my pregnancy. It was the worst thing I had ever done. I felt horrible about the choice I made. I would see babies and instantly wonder about my baby and what he or she would look like. It took a long time to let it go, and honestly it is something I've never totally gotten over. Eventually, I learned to forgive myself knowing that God loves and forgives me. I moved on and we went on hanging out with friends, partying and fighting. He continued to cheat, I continued to forgive. We would fight and argue and he would apologize, so I would forgive. I got pregnant a second time, and I miscarried shortly after discovering the pregnancy. I felt guilty and believed I was being punished for the abortion I had. Finally, I understood that our relationship was unhealthy and that we needed to let it go. I loved him way too hard, more than I loved myself.

I remember one night we drove to get one of his friends, who was a pastor, he had called to see if we could pick him up. He was conducting a revival. That phone call changed our life, briefly. We attended the services the entire week. It was on the last night of the revival, we gave our life to Christ. We wanted to be in alignment with God's word so we decided to get married and 9 months later the Lord saw fit to bless us again with our beautiful daughter. Our daughter was born with Down Syndrome. Most people would have been sad, but I can honestly say that I did not blame God, nor was I disappointed. I believed that she was truly a gift, and God chose to give us such a special blessing. Our daughter was blessing to our life and the lives of our families. We had a scare with a heart defect, they are common in children with Down Syndrome. At 17-month-old our daughter had open heart surgery. God saw fit to bless her and the surgery was a success. We tried to stay active in our church and follow God, but we soon found that old habits had found their way back into our life. We tried to make a go of it for the next several years but we just couldn't fix us. I needed to fix me. I finally got tired of the fighting, the sadness and dysfunction, so after 5 years, my second marriage ended.

However, I would soon be faced with another failed marriage. I thought to myself I had been married and divorced twice. I'm finally going to take the time I need to heal. I'm going to learn to love and appreciate the beautiful woman that I am. I was going find myself. I'm worthy of love. I will not jump into another relationship for a long time. I'm going to just do me.

It's better to marry than to burn. It had only been a month, and I met someone. I had been going out with friends, trying to keep busy and keep my mind off my 2nd failed marriage. I saw him around a few times before and thought he was good looking. He was tall, dark, and handsome. We went to breakfast that first night. We started right up, I hadn't even been separated 2 months and here I

100

was seeing someone else. I shared everything about all the ups and downs of my marriages. I shared the hurts and pains of my life from childhood to that present time. I even opened up about my hopes and dreams for the future. I could not believe that I was sharing the most intimate pieces of my life with him, even my secrets. I was so open and comfortable with him. He listened to me and we would talk for hours on end. He wanted to get to know my daughters and had two of his own. I thought he had to be the one that God sent to me, it seemed too good to be true.

The first red flag was that he lived with a friend and her kids, because he was a *little down on his luck*. He was working and trying to get on his feet so that he could move into his own place. So, after a few months he did move out, it lasted a couple months. His apartment was broken into and I allowed him to move in with me. I do not know how the topic of marriage came up again. He had never been married before and talked of his desire to marry and have a family. I was not even divorced yet and was starting to plan wedding number 3. I had to be losing my mind to be thinking about getting married again! So, I went to work on getting the divorce so I could walk down the aisle for the 3rd time. We participated in premarital counseling with our pastor, and I remember him saying we were not ready. I honestly started to see the warning signs shortly after we moved in together, but I ignored them because I wanted this to work. I knew that he was not right, but I wanted to prove to the pastor, my family and friends that they were wrong. So, one month after my divorce was final, I married yet again. It was not yet 6 months into the marriage, and the cycle was continuing. The arguing and fighting was getting worse with the onset of every marriage. I started to withdraw from my friends and family because he said we needed to establish us and our family. We did not need any outside interference, including my daughter's fathers who were very active in their lives, they were great dads. I disagreed with this and this is when the demise of the relationship started. There were many issues in the first few months. He would move in and out whenever things didn't go his way. He was very manipulative and was always finding something wrong with everything I did. I remember he would lecture me like a little kid for hours and I would just sit and listen, and agree. I was so sad when he would move out for a few months, instead of being happy that I didn't have to walk on pins and needles, I wanted him back. I did not realize it then, but I was getting accustomed to being abused and mistreated. The time apart did not bring us any closer together. It continued to go up and down for another year and he left again. This time he would not come back at least as my husband. We divorced after 17 months of marriage.

That did not, however mark the end of our relationship, we continued for 6 years more. I do not know why I just did not let it be over. I could not seem to let go. I still had so much love for him. I was always there for him when he needed me. He would start other relationships and when they ended he was running back. I was still there for him. I let him move back in when he lost his place and he stayed long enough to get on his feet, and then off he went again. He even remarried while still seeing me and when that ended in a few months there he was again. I was so focused on him and what he was doing that I was losing myself. I could not believe I was allowing this dysfunction to control my life. I lost my job because of all the stress. I was becoming someone that I did not know anymore. It was as if I had been rendered powerless to walk away from what I knew was not good for me.

This roller coaster went on for years. I must say it took a lot of praying and crying to finally let go of this relationship. It was one of the hardest things I ever had to go through. That relationship took me to many dark places in my life. My family and friends would say to me "when you've finally had enough," then you will walk away. It ended, I finally had enough. I still think back on that period in my life and often wonder how I walked away with my sanity. I was broken to the core by this relationship. If it had not been for God, my family and the love of my friends, I do not know if I could have made it through. I thank and praise God that I did.

So now the journey begins and it's just me and my youngest daughter. My oldest went off to college. I leaned on my friends a lot after this last relationship and would not have made it without their love and support. They loved and encouraged me when I did not know how to do it myself. I was often asked why I allowed myself to be subjected to such treatment and why I did not walk away. The fact is I did not know how to stand tall anymore. I allowed myself to disappear and I became someone that I did not recognize. I honestly never got the chance to fall in love with myself and was still learning who I was. I went from being a teenager to a wife. I never had the chance to be a kid. My self-esteem was gone and I did not realize my worth. I knew that I needed to get myself together and find a pathway to healing. It would not be easy and I can honestly say that I struggled for some time after that. I was starting to understand who I was the more time I spent alone. I needed to figure out what I liked about me. I decided to write in a journal. I would write about anything that would come to mind. I wrote about my pain and how what I went through made me feel. I wrote about the people that hurt me. I wrote about my day and how I was feeling. I wrote about how beautiful trees were and how fresh cut grass smelled. I couldn't wait for spring to see the flowers blooming. I loved how beautiful the trees were when they were full of green leaves. It was my way to deal with what I was feeling. The journal was my therapy, but I knew I needed more. I started to pray and talk to my father, the one who loved me unconditionally and the one who brought me through the storm. It was not long before I made my way back to church. I thanked God for the bishop's sermons. It was as if he had designed each one for me personally. I was encouraged and was starting to find peace during every service I attended. I remember one Sunday it was time for the altar call. The pastor and the choir were singing, "When the Spirit of the Lord" by Fred Hammond. I was flooded with joy, I started crying and praising, I lifted my hands and danced like David danced. There's part in the song where he says, "if you been through what I've been through excuse me neighbor I got to be dancing too!"

I found myself at the altar rededicating my life to God and taking yet another step to heal. I stopped being so hard on myself and took a moment to marvel at my life. I thought about the grief that softened me. I thought about the heartache that made me wiser, and the suffering that strengthened me. Despite it all, I'm still standing strong. I started changing some of the people I hung around, places I went, and things that I did in my life. I surrounded myself with the people that loved me, my friends and family. I talked about what I was feeling and stopped hiding everything inside. I forgave myself for not loving me and taking care of my own heart. I forgave myself for any pain that I caused the people in my life. The most important thing was forgiving those who hurt me. This was not an easy process but I grew stronger and stronger every day. With God's help, I could move past the pain. I was spending time with myself, and God was revealing his love for me and through the process I was starting to love me. I was beautiful and strong. I started seeing the good in myself. I was a good mother, daughter, sister, and friend. I did not have to accept conditional love anymore because my God loved me unconditionally! I could be free from all my pain because when I prayed, God promised me that he would always be there to wipe the tears from my eyes. I asked God to live big in me and to change the memories that caused such pain in my life and replace them with love and happiness.

It's been 17 years since my last marriage, I'm happy with my life. I have great friends that I love dearly and they love and support me. I travel more than I ever have and I'm having the time of my life. I have a job that I enjoy and great people in my life. I have both my parents in my life and I thank God for them. I have two awesome brothers and I want to one day marry a man like them. They are my heroes.

The best thing I ever done was to bring two amazing daughters into this world. I thank them for loving me and being my best friends. I might also, add they keep me young in heart and mind. I thank and praise God for all the storms of this life. I will continue my journey of healing and loving the life I have. While there are some things that I haven't been able to let go of completely, God is continuing to work on me and through me. I'm open to love and I believe that God is going to give me someone someday that I love and that will love me and together we will love and worship Him. I am not where I used to be, and I thank God in advance for what He's revealing to me even as I write this, my journey continues. I know that God is preparing me to be a blessing to other women by allowing me to go through and come out of the storm.

No matter your story, you can come out victorious!

About the Author

Sherri Hampton has had over 10 successful years in sales management with Cracker Barrel Old Country Stores, and was awarded Retail Manager of the year in 2010. She enjoys spending time with her family and friends. She is a daughter, sister, mother, grandmother and survivor. Sherri is compassionate, outgoing and has a true passion for life. She enjoys traveling and experiencing new adventures. Sherri loves listening to all genres of music and believes that music calms the soul. She enjoys reading quotes on life and wisdom, and writes poetry in her spare time. Inspiration comes from the love of family and friends that keep her rooted and grounded.

Sherri was born and raised in Decatur, Illinois. She currently resides in Champaign, Illinois with her youngest daughter.

FROM ASHES TO BEAUTY

by

Authrine T.K. Watson

Before I shaped you in the womb,
I knew all about you.
Before you saw the light of day,
I had holy plans for you:
A prophet to the nations—
that's what I had in mind for you.[7]

Reading and fully digesting Jeremiah 1:5 is exciting news my friend! It lets us know that regardless of what happens throughout the course of life, God already knows about it and we will still be who He created us to be. He saw us before our existence and He already knows our endings! *Whatever* we go through, it will be used to shape us into the destiny that God created for us! Regardless of failures, mistakes and mishaps, God has a purpose for our existence.

If you're anything like me, it took me a long time to realize this text. There were many storms in my life that I did not think that I would make it through. For instance, being raised in a single parent home in many ways made me feel

---

[7] **Jeremiah 1:5 The Message (MSG)**

inadequate and without identity. However, as I matured in life and in Christ, I understand that trials, tests and situations are great character developers. I stand in a place of strength today, but let me tell you, it was no easy journey! There were countless times I wanted to quit and stay stuck. But, I am so grateful I didn't. I am who I am, by the grace and mercy of God.

Though I am very optimistic today, primarily because of God's role in my life, I do want to share a portion of my life, where I have been, who I am today and where I am going. I hope you enjoy the journey!!!!

As an adult, whenever someone would ask how I was doing I would often respond, "I am fine, I will be okay"- regardless if that was the truth or not. As a child, I walked around with a frown on my face most of the time. I must have been tired of people asking me if I was ok or what was wrong with me because as an adult, my frown shifted into having a smile plastered on my face always. I would smile and fake like I was happy, but on the inside, I felt dead, and did not feel so great about myself. I really didn't know who I was and I was always trying to please people. I had suppressed my feelings for so long that most times, I didn't even know how to accurately label my feelings or emotions. I would quickly dismiss the feelings; often feelings of guilt emerged.

Growing up in a single parent home was very challenging and there were so many things that I did not understand as a child. I remember a lot of sad times, feeling like there was something missing because everyone I knew had their dad but I did not. Frowning and looking sad was my way of dealing with what was going on in my heart, mind and home. People would often say, "smile," or "what's wrong with you?" My own mother would even ask me the same questions. One time she said, "You act as if the weight of the world is on your shoulders." I remember responding to her, "I have nothing to smile about."

As a young child, I grew up in a home without a father, and my mother who worked really hard to make sure that everything we needed was provided. We had everything that we needed physically, but I lacked the emotional connection with my parents. My mom did the very best that she could taking care of four children. She wanted to be sure that her reason for coming to America would not be in vain. My mother attended nursing school while working full-time, she wanted to be sure we would have an example of success. My mother's drive for success caused her not to be at home as much as we needed.

Then, I was unable to express and externalize my feelings of not having my father consistently in my home. So, my outward expression of a frown mimicked the void that I felt in my heart. For a long time, I struggled feeling good about myself. I didn't know who I was and I longed for a relationship with my father. I always wanted to be a daddy's girl but wasn't, and that hurt. I have always loved my father and until this day, I still do.

When my father was in the home, he was a great father. I remember him telling us bedtime stories and making eggs with cheese for breakfast. Those were great times but I longed for more. I longed for a deeper relationship with my father. My father was supposed to be the one that told me I was beautiful, smart, and that I deserved the best. I didn't hear those things from my father. Fathers are the ones who give their children attention, validation and are the role models of healthy relationships. I did not get that, so I created my own version. The relationships I engaged in were faulty, unhealthy, and detrimental. So, with a father who was not around or invested in his children and a mother who was busy, I sought for attention. I thought that the attention from older men would fill the void of not having a father, but boy was I wrong. It caused more damage than good. My mother stayed and my father left. *It's unfortunate how the parent that remained in the home are typically the one who is forced to deal with all those misplaced emotions.* The void of not having a father manifested in anger and frustration in dealing with my mother. As a teenager, I didn't realize it, but I blamed my mother for my father leaving. It was not until I was in my 20's that I understood what was happening. It was then, I could start dealing with these thoughts and feelings. I had to be honest that the feelings were real. This was the start of the journey to healing and restoration.

My mother did the best that she could with what she had. She was a single parent with 4 children who came to America from Jamaica in the 1970's to make a better life for herself. I am the third child of four. You see my mother was married; she did it the right way. She was married but the marriage did not work out and so here she was struggling with 4 children. At the time, I didn't know it, but my mother was struggling emotionally to hold it together for her family. While my mother was trying to hold it together and to keep moving forward in life, I was experiencing struggles of my own.

There are so many stories that stand out in my mind between elementary and high school. I went to a private school so we were small. I remember this girl in junior high named "Amy". She was this skinny, caramel girl who had been taught in her home to be confident. Well, when low self-esteem meets confidence, a conflict was bound to happen. Man, I couldn't stand "Amy". She thought that she was all that and I thought that I was all nothing. I remember a terrible conflict I had with "Amy" and a few of us other girls. It was quite intense, as we were all pulled into the school office. I remember Amy saying to the group, "You all are just jealous because I'm prettier! You are jealous because you are fat, black and have short hair!" Even though she didn't personally call me out, I knew she was talking about me! She was right, I felt as if I had been cursed. I was fat, black and had short hair and glasses too! Before then, I had never really processed those feelings. I kept them bottled inside.

Due to my mother's intense schedule, I felt a disconnect from her. I really did not know how to process my feelings effectively. The times we did talk, I did not feel comfortable expressing to her my true feelings. Since I could remember, I was accustomed to keeping things to myself. I am not sure what started this trend, but it aided me in not dealing with my feelings.

However, by the time I was in high school, God used influential women that invested in my life and helped me to deal with some hard and challenging times growing up. Once, while I was in my guidance counselor's office during my sophomore or junior year, I discussed with her my feelings of inadequacy and frustrations of not feeling beautiful. Ms. Baker said, "You are beautiful and smart and God has a purpose for your life." We talked about my future and she stressed the importance of valuing who I was created to be. At the time, I would mostly listen and just held my head down. I didn't see myself as beautiful or smart because I didn't hear those words often, or in my home. I came from a good home, but my home was quiet. It was quiet from words of affirmation and validation. It was quiet from love and hugs. It was quiet from words like, "You're beautiful and you're smart." Because my home was quiet, my ears were more in tuned with words like, "You are ugly, you are fat, and you are not smart!" Soon, this low self-esteem opened the door to seek attention from older men. It was these older men that told me I was beautiful and they gave me that attention that my soul was starving to receive. I didn't have the foundation in my home, I was ashamed of who I was. When you do not know who you are you accept garbage from the enemy.

Overall, high school was rough. I went to a private small school until 8th grade and going to a larger high school was a huge adjustment. To make matters worse, there was a bully that seemed to make my days even more miserable. I was in the cafeteria, it was my junior year in high school (1996). I was eating lunch with my friends. I was wearing a yellow pullover rain jacket. My hair was freshly crocheted and I was wearing brown contact lenses. I was 100% confident, that I looked amazing that day! I sat there at the cafeteria table eating a sandwich with some french fries. I added my usual: ketchup, mayo and melted cheese (don't knock it until you try it ☺). I shared lots of laughs and was having a pretty good day. Things were well as I was hanging out with my friends in the cafeteria at Evanston Township High school. Then, out of nowhere Mr. T came up from behind and said, "What is that shi...in that jacket?" An explosion of laughter ensued. Immediately, I felt ashamed, embarrassed and alone. I left the cafeteria instantly and tried to stay out of his way as much as possible for the rest of the day. Though I tried to avoid him, it seemed to be his mission to find me. Thinking back, if I were just a tad more confident back then, I would have stood up for myself, and gave him a few choice words!

Anyway, God is hilarious. God is also sovereign and wise! A few weeks passed, and what was once relegated to school became a larger issue, so I thought. Originally, I would only see Mr. T at school, but one day things changed. I walked in church, and guess who I saw? You guessed it right, Mr. T! I thought to myself, "Really God, are you serious? Do you mean to tell me I have to see the tormentor, bullying, harassing man here too?" Well, thank God after numerous apologies and humility, I conceded and forgave him. Mr. T and I became good friends, even to this day.

Reflecting, I allowed people's views of me to be louder than the truth of who God created me to be. For a long time, I did not feel smart or beautiful. The Lord used another woman named Alana Amaker to affirm me. She too, was a staff member at my high school and that also attended my church. Ms. Amaker was a beautiful, chocolate woman who was very confident. She was integral in helping me to feel beautiful and to appreciate my dark (chocolate) skin. She also helped me to develop my sense of fashion. I went from wearing my brothers' baggy jeans to wearing short tight skirts (though she wasn't responsible for the length of my skirts, however, lol). She helped me become more confident about my beauty; however, I still struggled with feeling smart.

This feeling started a long time ago. I remember feeling this way as early as 2nd grade; not believing that I was intelligent enough. During kindergarten, I was held back, but I am not sure why. This meant that I would be the tallest and "thickest" person in 1st grade. This is where the seed of not feeling smart was planted. It persisted even to my college days. Once I made it to college I felt extremely inadequate and unintelligent. I remember asking a woman in the Financial Aid Office to tell me where the Special Education office was because I didn't believe I was fit for traditional classes. So, my mom and I went to the office and the person asked me had I ever taken any Special Education class, and I responded, "No". Then she asked me a series of other questions, to all of which I answered, "No." She said to me, "You do not qualify for Special Education services!" I left out of their office with great laughter on the outside, but I still felt deeply inadequate on the inside. Even though, according to their standards, I had the ability to achieve successfully in college, my confidence in myself was the missing and most important element. These feelings persisted even after completing my master level degree. I graduated high school early and even completed my master level degree in record time, but still felt unintelligent. Soon, I made peace, believing that God didn't make me smart and this would always be my struggle.

More recently, I was asked to speak at a church on the topic of self-worth. Immediately I thought that this is just like God. He will take the very thing that I struggled with and was ashamed about, and use it to help someone else. Understanding the great assignment, I begin to prepare for the speaking opportunity. I spoke with Ms. Amaker. I revealed to her that I still struggled with feeling smart. She reminded me it's not about being or feeling smart, but preparation was the most important thing. Smart is not what you are, but how you handle a situation. For instance, if math is an area of struggle, it would be smart and wise to invest more time studying and asking for help. Man, her perspective really blessed me! For so long I struggled with feeling smart. Soon I began to realize that everyone has struggles but it's how you handle the deficiencies and struggles that render you wise and smart.

It's funny how I remember these stories and I have been out of high school for over 20 years. The beauty of all of this, is I can reflect and there is no pain. This is truly God! The pain, the shame, the hurt and the ugliness is gone and what has been revealed is beauty. Isaiah 61:3, which says "To appoint them that mourn in Zion, to give them beauty for ashes, the oil of joy for mourning, the garment of praise for the spirit of heaviness; that they might be called trees of righteousness, the planting of the Lord, that he might be glorified." God told us he would give us beauty for ashes. Most times we go through things to shape our character and to propel us to our destiny so that God's plans can be completed. Romans 8:28 says, "And we know that all things work together for good to them that love God, to them who are called according to his purpose." All things work together, the good the bad and the ugly to fulfill God's plans for our lives. If I had not experienced these trials and storms, I wouldn't be the person I am today. My story brings glory to God, for I am no longer bound by issues that come from not having an absent father. I know my value and my worth! And my worth is in God!

I do want you to know that it hasn't been easy. Even as an adult, I still had battles with my identity. I would find myself being intimidated by people's strong personality. Often, I would compare myself or not be my true self, for fear of judgement or scrutiny. Not having my father had a negative impact on my relationships. I was always anxious and never trusted my judgement. My need for love of a man continued. I fell in love with the idea of a relationship than with the actual person. I recently learned I began to understand the root causes of my poor relationship decisions. Because of my own abandonment issues regarding my dad, I did not think that I was worthy of keeping or being pursued. The enemy wanted to use me not having a father to cause severe trauma in my life and leave me with a lasting void. As read earlier, this affected my confidence, my ability to love and allowed me to make very unwise decisions. It was the goal of the enemy to steal my innocence, he wanted to destroy my destiny and he wanted to kill my value.

It's amazing that the very thing that the devil tried to make me ashamed of, is the very thing that I love about myself. I love my chocolate skin. I never aspired to own my own business, but once I was healed from hurt I was certain that I wanted to invest in the lives of young ladies. I wanted

118

to pour into their lives just as others had poured into my own. I resolved, that every girl that I encountered, would know that she was smart, valuable and beautiful. It became my mission to plant those seeds. This commitment birthed *Glamour Girl (Masters Touch Salon)*. Isn't it amazing how God can use your brokenness and rough places to help someone else? Each day, I get to empower, inspire and encourage woman and girls as they sit in my chair. While I naturally work on their exterior, the Lord allows opportunities to plant seeds in their spirit. What an awesome God!

People look at me and tell me all the time how beautiful and gifted I am. Who would have known that God would take my scars and turn them into works of art? Only God the Creator of the universe could do that.

How did this healing happen you ask? So, glad you did! It was in my honesty that God that began to heal my esteem just like Adam and Eve. I needed to be open and naked in God's sight. For a long time, I felt guilty about my feelings because I felt that Christians shouldn't have those insecurities. God created me with feelings and he assured me he would still love me and could handle my feelings. In becoming healed and delivered from low- self-esteem, I have learned the following things:

1. ***Be honest with God-pray often.*** For a long time, I wouldn't deal with my feelings because I felt guilty and felt that Christian shouldn't have certain feelings. What I have learned and am learning is that God can handle our feelings and he will still love us. He told us to cast our cares on him for he cares for us. God

created us and he already knows how we feel. It is during the quiet time with God, that He can begin to speak to you and deal with your emotions. If you cannot verbalize them, write them down. Your feelings are natural and normal. The key is to not stay in your feelings. Talk about your feelings to God and to those you trust and move on. Don't get stuck in your feelings.

2. ***Ask God to heal your heart, hurt and esteem.*** God is a healer and He not only wants to heal you from physical diseases or sicknesses, but also from emotional scars and from not knowing who you are. Each day, I must ask God to search my heart and to create in me a clean heart. I want to have a heart like Jesus. He was betrayed, lied on, spit on and crucified and he took all of it, because of love and the bigger purpose-to die for our sins. Be patient, healing is a process, but it can be done. When issues arise, don't run from them. Instead confront them and ask the Holy Spirit to help you get rid of the residue. God created you and everything about you. Each of us has a purpose, gifts and talents that will help fulfill our purpose for existing. Don't compare yourself to anyone else; God knew exactly what He was doing when He created you. You are not here on accident, you are not a mistake but you are loved by the best-God. Like I tell my clients at the salon, "work with what you got." Everyone has something, get to know yourself. Know your strengths and work it.

3. ***Talk to people who will pray with you and be real.***
It is important to surround yourself with people who
hold you accountable. I have a great group of sisters
and my pastor in which I can discuss my issues and
feelings. My circle counsels, rebukes, advises,
encourages, and prays for me. It is not healthy to deal
with your feelings and emotions by yourself, but you
need people that you trust to help you deal with the
issues you face. There have been times when my
thinking was not good towards certain issues I was
struggling with, but my friends were able to use
wisdom and point me in the right direction.

4. ***Let God elevate you from where you are to where He
is calling you.*** God created you so He knows what
His plans are for your life. Often, we want to stay
stuck in our hurts and pains. We find it difficult to
move past our insecurities and frailties, but if God
called you, then you are capable and able. Don't put
yourself in a box. Don't let your past dictate your
present and your future. Rise to who God is calling
you to be. View yourself as Christ see's you. He calls
you beloved, he says you are royal, you are priceless.
You are in the palm of the Master's Hand. Girl, you
got it going on! Don't see yourself as the little girl
who was raped, mistreated, abused or neglected. See
yourself as wonderfully and fearfully made. See
yourself as being very good. For when God created
man, He looked at Him and said this is very good!

5. ***Re-affirm yourself daily through the word of God
   and affirmations.*** It would be awesome to say that I
   no longer struggle with low self-esteem but the truth
   is that each day I must make a choice to know who I
   am and to value Authrine T.K. Watson. To ensure
   that I don't forget who I am I do daily affirmations/I
   am statements. When the enemy brings bogus, nasty
   lies about my worth, I defeat those thoughts with the
   word of God and remind myself of where God has
   brought me from. I am a living testimony of God's
   grace and mercy. The enemy only attacks people that
   are a threat to him. The Bible says he walks around
   as a roaring lion seeking those he can destroy. He is
   not a roaring lion but he acts as one. Meaning he is a
   fake, a phony a pretender. If you listen to his roar
   and you look at him you will think he is a lion but he
   is not. The reality is that through Jesus Christ we
   have the power to overcome any identity crisis,
   because we have the greater one on the inside of us.
   We were bought with a price, we are priceless. We are
   the apple of God's eye. My prayer is that you would
   know who you are and always remember that you are
   priceless.

Getting to where I am today has been and is a journey. Each
day I make a choice to be whom God intended me to be. I
refuse to allow my past to dictate the promises that God has
ordained and destined for my life. I was created to be
excellent, fruitful, passionate and progressive. The pain that I
went through has pushed me. I will not let the pain be in

vain because I choose to give God the glory through walking in victory and in knowing who I am. Because of whose I am, I walk with my head held high. I look to God, my creator for validation. I hope that you commit to the same! Don't put your confidence in people, status or things, they are frail and faulty and will fail you every time. However, God's love never fails and He never fails. You can trust God with your identity, since He is the one that created and purposed you.

I AM LOVED

Affirmation

I was created in the image of Christ; therefore, my purpose and identity is found in Him. I am loved by God for I am written in the palm of His hand. I am a treasure, valuable and priceless. There is purpose and greatness inside of me. My value comes from God and He is the one that validates me. I am confident, bold, courageous, beautiful and intelligent. I am not bound by my past or my failures and my security is not wrapped in the hands of feeble man but in the Hands of Almighty God. My destiny and future has been written and I shall fulfill and accomplish all that God created me to be. I am more than a conqueror and I am not defeated by life's situations. I know who I am and I walk in excellence and determination. My mind is renewed and my heart is clean. I am healed, whole and anointed to prosper. I am the head and not the tail above and not beneath and whatsoever I do shall prosper. I am a living testimony of God's goodness and mercy. I am the heir of Abraham and I am blessed. I am loved by God and His Love never fails.

About the Author

Authrine T.K. Watson is a young woman whose entrepreneurial spirit is made more inspiring by her desire to help others recognize the greatness that they each possess. Using her salon, Master's Touch in Bloomington, IL as a platform, Authrine has connected her heart to please God with her passion for uplifting others. This dynamic combination of passion and purpose has led Authrine on a unique journey to become an advocate and community resource for young women as well as foster and adoptive children and their families.

With her faith in God to sustain her, and Proverbs 16:3 (*Commit your actions to the Lord, and your plans will succeed.*) to propel her, Authrine has set forth on a mission to enrich the lives of the young people she encounters. She has put her gifts, skills and talent to work abroad -- doing missions work in the Bahamas, Africa, the Philippines and Guyana -- and locally, as the creator of community outreach programs like Beauty of Hope and Glamour Girl.

Drawing on more than 10 years of experience in the field of social work, Authrine introduced Beauty of Hope after seeing a growing need for caregivers to be educated on how to properly care for and maintain the health of children's hair and skin. By way of classes and one-on-one consultations, Beauty of Hope has been instrumental in helping foster and adoptive children develop the self-esteem necessary to preserve their culture and to realize who they were created to be.

As a hair stylist, Authrine has made it her mission to make young ladies feel beautiful inside and out. She has carried out this mission through Glamour Girl, a series of self-esteem and empowerment seminars held annually in Illinois. Designed for girls ages 10-18, Glamour Girl offers attendees inspiration, candid conversation on topics like the importance of engaging in healthy relationships, and practical advice on how to achieve academic and financial success.

As she continues to lay out her plans to instill hope, and inspire young girls to grow into confident young women, Authrine's primary desire is for God to be glorified in all that she does.

Authrine is a graduate of Illinois State University, and holds a B.S.W and M.S.W in Social Work. She is a native of Evanston, IL and currently resides in Bloomington, IL. Authrine is a member of City of Refuge Ministries under the leadership of Sr. Pastor William Bennett.

9

MY HEART'S DESIRE
by
Anna Koomalsingh

The day had finally arrived! Things were so perfect, I could just pinch myself! A fairytale wedding. It was a day all girls dreamed would come true. From the time I was 6 years old, I imagined the details of this day. I knew who would be there, what I would wear, all of it! "Here comes the bride, all dressed in white, da da da daaa da da da da daaa!"

The courtship was eleven years; together we worked hard to get to this day. All the day's plans were perfectly set. Everything fell into place exactly the way I had imagined. I remember sliding into my long sequin Mermaid gown and slipping on my elegant jeweled shoes. Oh, I felt like a modern-day Cinderella! How proud and taken by my beauty, my groom would be as I floated up the aisle to meet him at the altar.

It all began when my father came to this country at the age of eighteen with $50 on a student visa. He worked during the day and attended classes at night. It was during that time that he met my mom at a college party. According to my mom, it was love at first sight. We were a small family of five (my parents, my older sister, younger brother and me).

We resided in a two-bedroom brick Georgian-style home. Our extended family here in America was quite small, so we relied on one another. We did not have much, but for all intents and purposes, I would consider us middle-class. My dad was self-employed and left the house in his truck every morning to earn a living as a service technician. Our family style was simple and uncomplicated. We were raised to be down to earth kids. We each completed our individual household chores with the usual childish complaints. But no matter what, we all knew that when we heard my dad give his truck one last rev, it was lights, camera and action! Every pillow on the couch was checked to ensure placement, garbage was taken out, dad's food was warmed up, and his place was perfectly set at the table. After all, each of us had our role in the family and we had to do our part to make our family work effectively.

We were blessed to have two loving parents to watch over and provide guidance. They were serious advocates of education. They sacrificed a lot to provide the three of us with a private education from elementary through graduate school.

My identity and self-esteem were strongly linked to my father's vision of success for us. His sense of approval was significant for me, as it became a driving force in my life. If we concentrated on our studies and abstain from the topic of *boys*, things ran smoothly. We understood that our parents only wanted the very best for our family and were strong advocates for our success. My dad was an advocate for the *American Dream*.

Dad was very overprotective of my sister and I. Talking to a male friend, let alone having a boyfriend was a first-class ticket to an early grave. "Better not get caught," was a familiar chant of my "goodie, goodie" sister. Well, I did get caught a couple of times for coming home well after curfew.

At 21, I finally found the courage to come clean and tell my father how I felt about this man I had dated for so long. You see, he picked me out of all the hundreds of girls in my all girls high school year book. I could hardly believe it when my friend, Laura stopped by my house one hot August evening. At first I thought, "how nice was it for her to want to come and see me after my month-long trip to Trinidad." I thought she wanted to hear all about the delicious curried meals and the fine Trini men. But after the usual chit chat she quickly took our conversation in another direction. She told me a close male friend of hers was outside in the car and wanted to meet me. Talk about being confused! In disbelief, I asked Laura, "Who would want to meet me?" And of all things, my parents were seated on the living room couch in front of the opened door. I retorted, "Oh no! This is not an option, especially not tonight!" While I was flattered, I was not interested in the drama that was guaranteed if my father found out. I told her, "thank you, but let's discuss this at school next week." After all, I thought, "If he was *that* interested he would wait."

After the numerous and lengthy phone conversations after school for about a month, I finally decided it was worth the risk to meet him in person. After all, I was really impressed by his knowledge of The Word of God, the *Holy*

Bible. You see, even though I had a Catholic school education, I somehow felt that sense of connection was missing. It was not enough for me to recite the *Prayer of the Rosary* or recite ten *Hail Mary's* after confessions, I yearned for something more! I was beginning to question the very existence of God because I could not seem to make sense of it all. The insight and connection with him did not begin to come alive until our very talks about God being the foundation of all things and the inspiration of our heart's desires. Listening to *My Sweet* guy quote scripture and apply them to daily life, left me in awe as I found myself discovering the beauty and mysteries of this blessing called life. Each conversation was like hearing an unheard melody. So, yes, I made strategic plans to finally meet and visit him at his home.

I remember that day well. I was prepared for the weather that day. I wore a pair of black; flare legged polyester slacks, a t-shirt and a hooded multicolored striped sweater from *Sears*. I was equipped with my umbrella ready to greet the raindrops as I disembarked from the #8 Halsted street bus. I was nervous as I walked the 4 long blocks to his home. Not only was I going to meet him but his family too! I hoped my hair was still intact and had not frizzed up too much. I smoothed it down with one hand as much as I could while holding my umbrella in the other. "Oh well, it would just have to do," I said. Soon, I ascended the steps that led to the front door of his house. I took a deep breath and rang the doorbell. The door opened and shortly afterwards he appeared. This gorgeous, six foot, basketball playing dude greeted me with such a warm smile. He uttered in a deep tone

"Hi. You made it!" For a moment, it seemed like time stood still. All I remember was feeling my heartbeat in sync with the symphony of falling raindrops upon my umbrella. He opened the door and motioned me to enter. But first, I turned my back to him, shook my rain drenched umbrella out, and put on a smile as wide as the Panama Canal. All the while I thought to myself "Oh my God, I hit the jackpot!"

And did I say gorgeous? I turned back around, but not before putting my poker face back on. Of course, I couldn't let him know what I was really thinking. I certainly did not want to play a part in inflating his ego nor risk appearing frantic or desperate. I was a simple, kind hearted girl. He knew he looked good. My friend told me how girls went "gaga" over him on regular basis. Looks are by no means everything. Just like my mom used to always say. "God don't like ugly and He sure ain't crazy 'bout pretty!" Though I was in the clouds, the mental note was heeded. Could this really be true? Could I have really found my Prince Charming?

Well, maybe my Prince wasn't as charming as I first thought. Perhaps I wasn't as enchanting as he thought either. We each learned much about ourselves, our similarities and, of course, our individual differences during our lengthy relationship. The most important part for me was that I always felt that he was my friend and in being true friend, we could handle anything together. *My Sweet* went away to college while I chose to live on campus at the nearby university. We developed short-lived love interests during those college years, only to break up and make up. He gave me a "promise" ring. That was the next best thing to an engagement ring or at best better than the prize you get out of the Cracker Jack box! Ok, but I saw the bigger picture or, so I thought. After all, we were in our 20's and managed to carve out good careers for ourselves. We were inching closer and closer to a solid future. I knew he was a good catch and all but, so was I!

Now, going back to my long-awaited day, there was a special feeling in the air. The weather forecast predicted a chance of showers. A few lightly sprinkled the ground on the way to the church. Some would have taken that as a bad sign but, not me. Everything was a blessing from above and all things worked for the good of all. After all, it was *my* day - a day where all my dreams would become a reality. It was going to be my fairy tale with a blissful ending written by the Almighty Himself! Yes, that's what I've been asking for in my prayers. I so desired to get closer to the Lord and have that relationship of closeness and solidarity and sense of peace in my life. Yes, I had a sense of entitlement because I was a "good girl". I reached my educational goals and my career was taking off. The next items on the list: marriage and family.

Perfect, I surely was not and never professed to be. I attended an all-girls high school and for the most part it was a good experience. I did not think of myself as being stuck up but maybe that's how I appeared to others. I was more of an introvert finding her way amongst the crowd. It was the occasional female cruelty though, fueled by jealousy that seemed to teach the same redundantly painful lesson time and time again. Words really can hurt. Those lessons began during the middle school years. Sure, I can look back on them as

130

some real growing pains back then, but I was a victim of some real cruelty. There were some real lessons of survival of the fittest. For me, there was nothing worse than being around a bunch of females or cliques. They simply talk too much about...nothing! Well, this time they could talk about me. In fact, I did not mind news of my wedding day being that day's topic of conversation.

And so, to be married and raise a family was also my heart's desire. During high school, I often found myself in class doodling in my notebook and trying on the different sizes of my soon to be married name. I battled losing my identity, so I would need to decide if I would give up my last name all together, or go with the hyphenated version. It had been my prayer that God bless us with three children, just like both of our parents. The number three signified the *Holy Trinity* and how Jesus was the Way, the Truth, and the Life (John 14:6). I sat in class and doodled repeatedly. I had even picked out my would-be children's names! My heart confirmed what I felt was God's plan coming to fruition. After all, the Spirit must have led *My Sweet* to select my picture from that yearbook. However, not everyone was as certain as me.

The day had commenced. As we sat in the *Jaguar* limousine parked in front of the church, my father turned to me and lovingly asked, "Are you sure you really want to do this? You don't have to you know. We can just drive off." A father's love endures forever. I turned to him and replied "Daddy, I'm ready."

As those heavy wooden doors opened in front of my father and I, I could not contain my excitement. The church

131

was aglow with pink and white roses accented by long silver ribbons. The groomsmen stood handsomely dressed in all-black formal tuxedos. They resembled knights in black armor. They complemented the groom, dressed in his white formal double breasted tuxedo jacket and black designer trousers. One by one, each groomsman met and escorted each unique vision of iridescent beauty after gliding down the aisle to the instrumental melody of Quincy Jones' *Setembro*. Each unique beauty moved like a gentle whisper leaving her scent that marked her presence, like a fragrant candle. Standing alongside the Maid of Honor and the Best Man were five bridesmaids and five groomsmen along each side of us. Five were chosen to signify the number of God's grace. I remember turning to *My Sweet* and looking into his beautiful brown eyes. I thought, "I met a boy whom I would later call my friend, and who would in a moment become my husband." Together, we would find favor in the Lord.

I said, "I Do!" "Whoso findeth a wife findeth a good thing, and obtaineth favour of the Lord" (Proverbs 18:22), said the preacher. "I now pronounce you husband and wife. You may now kiss the bride." Immediately I thought, "Oh Lord, what have I done?"

I did not go into marriage with the belief that the perfection exhibited on our wedding day would be what resembled the marriage. Many advised us that with marriage there were going be many peaks and valleys along the way. There would be no way to predict how when or where, but *together*, we could weather any storm. But what would happen when the *we* become *me*?

We had a wonderful honeymoon aboard a cruise ship with other young honeymooners. However, two months in, it seemed like the fairytale ended abruptly. I thought it would have lasted at least a year! In my experience, women usually receive the bad reputation for things changing after marriage. But in our case, it was different. It was him! Suddenly, it was as if things literally changed overnight. All I knew was that I was his wife and he was my husband. We would take care of each other. We made this newfound commitment in the presence of the Lord, our family and our friends. I was in for the long haul.

From my lips to his ears were petitions of strength and wisdom. By no means was I naïve. I somehow knew a storm was brewing: the all familiar battle between the natural and the spiritual. I had watched enough soap operas, talked to enough married women and could bear witness to my mother's suffering and tears not to recognize the signs. I had the sense that maybe he was having regrets. I needed to brace for it. He was always very sociable and went out with his friends. I was the opposite and did not like to frequent outings. I did not have the power to change him. He spent less and less time with me; eventually, having increasingly late night to early morning returns home. Asking's turned into pleadings, as I desperate to confront the "elephant" in our marriage. It did no good. I kept asking myself, "What did I do wrong?"

One evening as he was about to leave I kept trying to talk with him until he turned and looked me in the eyes and said emphatically, "I'm going out wherever I wanna go and there's nothing you can do to stop me!" Sadly, he was right. I watched him get into his red sports car and back out of our driveway without giving me a second glance. What a lonely feeling! Soon, I heard the phone ring. The sound of the ring helped me to snap out of my disbelief. I rushed into the house to answer the phone. "Hello, Hello?" Calls followed by hang ups happened repeatedly and persisted quite frequently. This time, before the hang up I said, "If you're calling for him, he's not here. Why do you keep calling?" Her reply was "Girlfriend, you just don't know!" After those words, she abruptly ended the call. Click! Well, apparently, I did not know, but her words served as an open invitation to find out.

Stunned, I could feel my heartbeat thumping in my ears. My hands were trembling with rage and fear all at once. All I knew was that I was just insulted and disrespected on so many levels. She was dying to say something. She had her chance and she took it! It was if she was yelling a childlike, "Nah, nah na, nah, nah!" I felt utterly helpless! I was open, wide open, yet again. It was becoming increasingly painful to tolerate. But I had to see the truth for myself. You see, the caller ID feature had just hit the market. It was our modern-day GPS. As I trembled with fear, I soon found my way to her home. I had always heard stories that were liken to the one I was living. They *all* had horrible endings! However, my goal was certainly not to hurt anyone, but rather to see the truth for myself. I needed to do this. I was certain I would find him there.

I pulled up and suddenly, my mouth began to water and I became sick to my stomach. My eyes relayed the message to my brain, "confirmation received!" As I pulled up, I was startled to know that the exact car that sat in our

134

driveway not an hour before, was now parked right in front of another woman's home. As I drove around I came down the alley to see if I could get a glimpse of him, but all I saw were two garbage cans next to a black car. I circled around the block and parked my car and thought to myself, "do you really need to see some more? How much more humiliation do you require?" I was finally settled in the fact that I was there, so I confronted my fears. After all, I needed to let him know that he was not as smart as he thought nor could he continue to hurt me in this way! I just wanted the truth and no more games. I bowed my head and asked the Lord in prayer to order my steps and my words. With a deep breath, I got out of my car and proceeded to her doorstep. I took three steps and I was on her porch. I peered into the door's window and saw the two of them. WOW! What a vision? My husband was sitting in another woman's living room, holding a bottle of beer.

From that distance, a *Chicago Bull's* basketball game played as they were engrossed in their conversation. As they talked and laughed, there I stood on the other side of the door. It was me who felt like an outsider- the *OTHER* woman! She was stealing my treasures, but in truth he freely gave them; laughter, smiles, his time, his energy, his love, *himself*. Heaviness suddenly overcame me; my heart became heavy. What else did I need to help confirm that fact that the love of my life had betrayed and dishonored me? Before my brain could fully process the response, I felt the pressure of my fingertip upon the dimly lit doorbell. Startled, the starry-eyed couple looked toward my direction. Our eyes met. Denial of this moment was impossible! I heard him say to her, *she* is here! This woman came to the door and began speaking to me through the door as he walked out of sight's view. I asked her to send him out and she stated I must have made a mistake. She said, "his car is here, but he went out with my boyfriend." Wow, I could tell her IQ was really off the charts. I told her to just let him know that his wife would be waiting outside for him! I returned to my car and waited, and waited and waited. I knew there was no way he would ever leave his apple red, 300ZX with the shiny rims and T-tops in front of her house. Besides, he would need it to make a fast getaway. I waited and waited and waited some more. I've been told that patience is a virtue. Yes, I truly learned that in just one night! Finally, he came out, but from the back of her house. Again, he underestimated me because I was already sitting back there. I knew him. After eleven years, we knew each other's' thoughts and anticipations. As he took a few steps away from her house, I turned on the engine, shifted the gear into *drive* and firmly pressed the gas. I came to my sense within an inch of his kneecaps! He still denied that our eyes ever met. He was lying to me, to her and mostly to himself. With the shaking of my head, I asked myself "Why?" Was I not attractive enough? Was I not intelligent enough? **WHAT COULD I POSSIBLY HAVE DONE TO DESERVE THIS?**

That night we returned to our home as two different people than when we left. We had just suffered a major collision- the fatal kind. Our marriage was in intensive care and on life support. I knew he was hurting too but honestly, I did not care. No doctor could prescribe medications to take away this kind of pain. Eventually, I fell to my knees and just started to pray.

Prayer became a lifestyle for me. I remember thinking "there is nothing prayer can't overcome." I needed to gather my thoughts. I needed to hear the Word in His house so that I could eventually find peace in my own. *I needed to plan how to first save myself as I was accountable for my own actions, not those of others*. I needed to educate myself in the Word of God.

Beyond church attendance, I had to learn true forgiveness. Forgiveness is the best gift but also one of the hardest to give to oneself and others. So, I needed to be kind to myself for there was a long list of words to describe the feelings that I felt were stamped upon my forehead for all to see: STUPID, DUMB, NAÏVE, USED, INFERIOR, DESPERATE, or just plain *CRAZY!* I needed to give myself time to move through and to find the best route for this healing process to occur. They say confession is good for the soul. So, it is through *this* writing that I allow myself to continue healing.

In all, there are so many more details to my journey, but I will use another book to share many more lessons such as this one. However, my story is one like many others. No one ever hopes to have their dreams shift into a nightmare. I had hoped that my marriage would be healthy and happy. But through it all, I discovered some very key principles. I hope some of them will enlighten you in your own journey. The most importance lesson I want to include here:

- *Happiness* is a relative concept based upon a sense of personal fulfillment. We must first learn to seek a unique sense of happiness from within rather than from someone or something else. I learned the importance of finding myself on my own map of happiness especially in the midst of battle. For me, I received an even greater gift from my most personal wound, for it has always been my heart's desire to receive an even deeper understanding of God's *unconditional love* for the Word of God is the absolute truth!

My heart's desire was originally a beautiful marriage, but through a failed marriage He renewed my heart to desire His word. I am forever grateful! In fact, I have attached one of my favorite verses. Use it as a daily reminder of who you should be and represent.

1 Corinthians 13:4-8 (NIV)

[4] Love is patient, love is kind. It does not envy, it does not boast, it is not proud. [5] It does not dishonor others, it is not self-seeking, it is not easily angered, it keeps no record of wrongs. [6] Love does not delight in evil but rejoices with the truth. [7] It always protects, always trusts, always hopes, always perseveres.
[8] Love never fails. But where there are prophecies, they will cease; where there are tongues, they will be stilled; where there is knowledge, it will pass away.

About the Author

Anna Koomalsingh, received her BA in Psychology from the University of Illinois at Chicago and MS in Public Service Management from DePaul University. She has spent most of her career in Child Welfare Services working with children and their families. She has been a Foster/Adopt PRIDE Master Trainer for over 12 years with the Illinois Department of Children and Family Services (IDCFS) and is currently employed in Higher Education. The concept that children learn what they live is one she emphasizes in the classroom and takes to heart.

This faith-filled woman has always chosen to see beyond the surface, choosing to view challenges as opportunities for success. Viewing personal imperfections as an impetus to spiritual growth, she shares her pursuit to understand the natural and spiritual battleground onto which she found herself. She unveils the raw emotions of betrayal, vulnerability and courage while dispelling the myths of eternal brokenness and shame. During this test of integrity, she discovered the beauty of a relationship with God and His *Unconditional Love*. She provides encouragement to those seeking elevation despite all the presenting challenges. Finding the courage to do the right thing may seem a lonely road but never traveled alone for lessons of integrity must be lived to be taught.

When not helping others, Anna loves spending time with family and friends. She is the proud mother of three children. You can find her enjoying the tranquil presence of nature whether in her back yard or along her many domestic or international travels.

10

IT'S A WRAP

It is my prayer and hope that you have been inspired enough by the *Women of Ushindi* to write your story. We have all experienced devastating life events that crushed our inner being. Sometimes, we were able to bounce back quickly and other times not so much. I ask you to put on your brave hat and share your *U.G.L.Y.* story with someone. You never know whom you will touch. The stories shared in this book, in which some would call testimonies, were shared in an effort to provide hope; provide an example of how to overcome, and to convey to someone that they are not alone in their dark place. We hope we have been effective in achieving this goal. If so, we pray that you are able to share your own journey. It may be a bit uncomfortable at first, but ultimately it is a liberating experience! Become a Woman of Ushindi!!!

WOMEN OF USHINDI

I am spiritually connected to each of the women featured in this book, making the writing of this book a divine connection. One in particular, Cynthia, works with me and during a meeting she shared with her colleagues and I how she was robbed while leaving the county hospital in Chicago and how the only thing that upset her about the robbery was that the robber called her *ugly*. Her comment resonated in my spirit and days later while in the shower, I heard that quite still voice say, "Tell Cynthia she has to tell her story and you will create the platform for her to do so." I dropped the soap and looked around, even though I already knew there was no one in the bathroom but me. I also knew it was God speaking to me. Scripture says, according to John 10:5 that "My sheep know my voice and a stranger they will not follow. I instantly began praying and confirming what God had spoken. Days later, I asked Him how to proceed. I was instructed to reach out to Cynthia and tell her the "Good News." In doing so, she said, "If my story can help someone, I'm all in and would be honored." This conversation took place in November 2016, and this book was published and became a reality in April 2017.

After Cynthia agreed to write a chapter, I began to pray and ask God for the title of the book and instructions on how the book was to be laid out. In December, He gave me the title of the book, *U.G. L.Y., Uncovering God's Love for You: Stories of Triumph of Low Self-esteem and Self-worth*. I couldn't believe it! I pulled myself together and began to mediate on the title for a few more days or maybe even weeks. I went back to God and asked for the names of the other women who needed to share their story and literally within in minutes their faces began to appear before me. I saw Tina, Sherri, Jataun, Barbara, and several others who later declined due to personal circumstances. I went back to God and petitioned Him again for great clarity; soon, Genesis, Authrine, and Anna were confirmed. I set up a group *Instant Message* so we could begin communicating and I called us "Women of Influence." We had a conference call in which each of these women introduced themselves and shared a snippet of their story. After hearing their introductions, I realized they had triumphed over some emotionally and physically devastating obstacles and I wanted the name of our group to reflect that. I have a afro-centric flare, so I looked up the Kiswahili word for triumph, which is Ushindi. The word also means victorious. Ushindi described who we were, hence, we became the Women of Ushindi.

I leave you with some quotes that have helped me as I worked to become Ushindi!

The strong survive, but the courageous triumph. -Michael Scott

The harder the conflict, the more glorious the triumph. What we obtain too cheap, we esteem too lightly; it is dearness only that gives everything its value. I love the man that can smile in trouble, that can gather strength from distress and grow. -Thomas Paine

Whatever is bringing you down, get rid of it. Because you'll find that when you're free....your true self comes out. -Tina Turner

44885734R00087

Made in the USA
Middletown, DE
19 June 2017